Beyond
Sportdiving!

D1450516

Beyond Sportdiving!

Exploring the

Deepwater

Shipwrecks

of the

Atlantic

——

——

By Bradley Sheard

Menasha Ridge Press   Birmingham, Alabama

Copyright © 1991 by Bradley Sheard
Published by Menasha Ridge Press
First edition, second printing
Printed in the United States of America

Library of Congress Cataloging-in-Publication Data
Sheard, Bradley, 1958-
   Beyond sportdiving: exploring the deepwater shipwrecks of the
Atlantic/by Bradley Sheard.
   p.   cm.
   Includes bibliographical references and index.
   ISBN 0-89732-105-7
   1. Scuba diving—Atlantic Coast (U.S.) 2. Shipwrecks—Atlantic
Coast (U.S.) I. Title.
VM989.S44 1991
622'.19'0916346—dc20   91-13900
                                                               CIP

Menasha Ridge Press
3169 Cahaba Heights Road
Birmingham, Alabama 35243

To my grandfather,
Henry Oscar Nilsson,
who first
introduced me
to ships and the sea,
and provided the spark
from which
all else has followed.

———
———

Life is
a daring adventure,
or nothing at all.
—Helen Keller

Contents

Acknowledgments

During the course of writing this volume, by necessity I conducted much needed research by mail. The institutions and individuals with whom I corresponded were of invaluable assistance, and much of what I have written would have been impossible without their generous help. I would like to extend my gracious thanks to all, and to thank in particular the following organizations:

City of Dundee District Council, Art Galleries and Museums, Dundee, Scotland

The Federal Court of Canada
Guildhall Library, Aldermanbury, London
Kendall Whaling Museum, Sharon, Massachusetts
The Mariners' Museum, Newport News, Virginia
Ministry of Defence, London
Mystic Seaport Museum, Mystic, Connecticut
The National Maritime Museum, Greenwich, London
The Naval Historical Center, Washington, D.C.
New Bedford Free Public Library, New Bedford, Massachusetts
Old Dartmouth Historical Society Whaling Museum, New Bedford,
    Massachusetts
The Peabody Museum, Salem, Massachusetts
The Public Archives of Canada
Public Record Office, England
The United States Coast Guard
The United States National Archives

I would like to thank Theano Nikitas for many hours of careful editing and review of the manuscript and Professor Henry Keatts for his advice and encouragement throughout the creation of this volume, and special thanks to Chicki Guglieri for her help in translating from German the war diaries of the *U-117*, *U-151*, and *U-123*.

Captain George Hoffman provided important material and insights into the pioneering days of diving, as well as excellent charters aboard the *Sea Lion*. The charter services of the following dive boat captains is gratefully acknowledged, as it has made diving these wrecks a reality: Captains Steve Bielenda and Janet Bieser of the R/V *Wahoo*, Captain Billy Deans of the *Key West Diver*, Captains John Lachenmeyer and Frank Persico of the *Sea Hawk*, and Captain Bill Nagel of the *Seeker*.

I would like to thank Mike deCamp and George Hoffman for permission to use some of their excellent photographs in this volume.

Perhaps most of all, I would like to thank the Atlantic Wreck Divers, my close friends and companions throughout all of the adventures described herein, as well as many others.

Preface

———

This book is about adventure; real life adventure lived by ordinary people of average means from all walks of life. While these are ordinary people, they are extraordinary divers—easily the top one percent of their peers and probably better. The diving depicted here is well beyond the limits recommended by all sportdiving organizations and, in fact, beyond the range of scuba for almost all commercial, government, and military organizations. This type of diving is, in a word, *dangerous.*

It is not the intent of this work to encourage or recommend diving activities outside the guidelines established by recreational diving certification agencies, but rather to allow the ordinary layman and conventional sportdiver a glimpse at a fascinating world that would otherwise go unseen. It is also an exploration of the rich history behind each of these shipwrecks; for to those of us who dive them, this history is just as important as the adventure of exploring their remains.

It is my hope that through words and pictures I might convey an image of this forbidden, deep-sea world to those who will never have the chance to see it firsthand, and in so doing, perhaps enrich their lives as mine has been.

Beyond

Sportdiving

_____

_____

_____

_____

_____

_____

_____

_____

_____

_____

_____

_____

_____

_____

_____

_____

Shipwrecks are my life. I live, dream, think, and breathe shipwrecks. I have come to love them, and exploring their often tattered and broken bones has become my passion. But I am not alone. There are a handful of men and women who share my obsession, and collectively we explore their captivating remains and attempt to uncover their fascinating stories.

Recorded here in both pictures and words are all that remain of a few of the tragedies of man's seafaring past. But the sea, which so unforgivingly engulfed them at the moment of their surrender, has transformed them into a thing of beauty. They live on, now an incredible haven for a seemingly infinite variety of marine life. To visit such places, to explore and see what only a few will ever experience generates inspiration and awe. It is a spectacle never to be forgotten.

As beautiful as this world is, it is but half the adventure—for each broken ship has its own story, a rich history waiting to be uncovered and told to a world that has long since forgotten. Often this history is obscure and difficult to trace, buried deep in some dusty archive with only the barest of clues left to uncover its secrets. Many long hours have been spent by numerous individuals in the attempt to uncover the deep heritage of the shipwrecks contained herein, as well as the countless more that dot the sea floor. It is a labor of love by those whose very existence seems inexplicably tied to a long-forgotten world they feel compelled to resurrect and to understand. Far beneath the sea, the past and the present come together as one, and we have been allowed to touch them both.

From man's earliest beginnings he has gazed in wonderment at the oceans, curious about what lay beneath their waves. But his physiology prevented him from venturing too far into what is for man a hostile environment—only his persistence and ingenuity has allowed him to discover its secrets. It was the invention of the Aqua-lung in 1943 by Gagnan and Cousteau that brought the underwater realm to the doorstep of the common man. For the first time, man could swim about in the depths almost effortlessly—for a short period of time he could become as at home beneath the ocean as the fish.

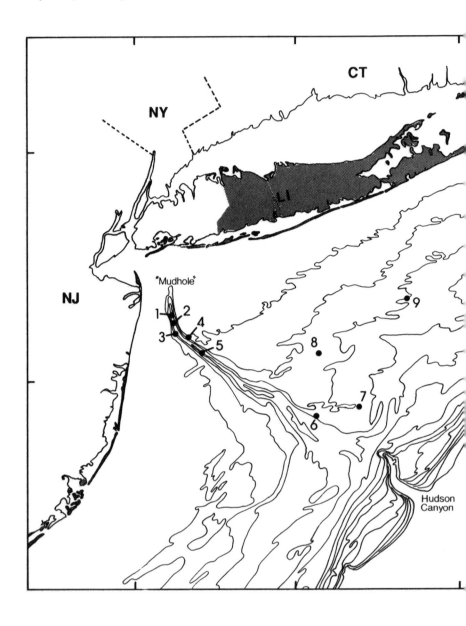

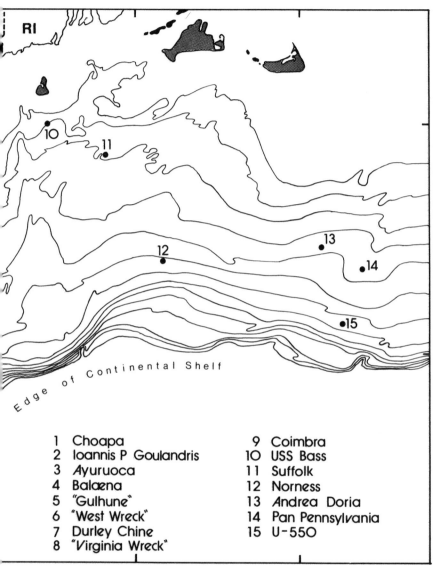

1	Choapa	9	Coimbra
2	Ioannis P Goulandris	10	USS Bass
3	Ayuruoca	11	Suffolk
4	Balæna	12	Norness
5	"Gulhune"	13	Andrea Doria
6	"West Wreck"	14	Pan Pennsylvania
7	Durley Chine	15	U-550
8	"Virginia Wreck"		

This bathymetric chart of the ocean floor off the New York and New Jersey coasts shows the location of some of the deeper shipwrecks in the area. Note the ancient river bed stretching from the "Mudhole" at the entrance of New York Harbor to the edge of the Continental Shelf and the Hudson Canyon. Drawing by author.

In the beginning, diving was only for the hardiest and most adventurous souls. Equipment was often homemade and difficult to use. But slowly, as better equipment became increasingly available, diving became more and more popular as a hobby for weekend explorers and adventurers. Diving clubs sprang up everywhere as the number of sportdivers slowly but steadily grew.

Today, diving has become a booming business. It is a self-regulated industry that sets its own standards and rules; there are no government licenses required to go scuba diving. All that is necessary is to take a four- to six-week course offered by one of the nationally recognized agencies (such as NAUI, PADI, or YMCA) in which you are taught the basic physical effects diving has on your body and how to handle yourself underwater. A certification card issued by one of these agencies is required to buy gear, to have air tanks filled, or to go out on a charter dive boat. Thus the industry polices itself, and the system works. Diving is a safe and enjoyable sport that can be enjoyed by almost anyone who is fairly comfortable in the water.

This is sportdiving—recreational diving that can be enjoyed by all who wish to try it. As defined by the certification agencies, sportdivers are limited to a maximum depth of 130 feet, and all are taught never to pass beyond this boundary. This is a sane and safe approach for the general public; diving becomes much more complicated at greater depths, and much caution and planning are involved in making deeper dives. But these agencies have in recent times taken to denying the existence of any activities beyond the scope of their teachings. This was not always the case. A journey through the pages of early issues of *Skin Diver Magazine* will quickly reveal tales of just such adventures.

Somewhere along the road between then and now, attitudes have changed. For the modern day sport scuba diver, there is no world below 130 feet—it does not exist. This is what we have been taught, and most accept it as gospel. But by its very nature, such a universal limit is purely arbitrary—a convenient depth that was chosen and declared safe, and beyond which lies risk and danger. But to preach that it is safe for no one to venture beyond 130 feet is just as absurd as to state that *anyone* can dive to 130 feet safely. People are not created equal—individual capabilities vary widely in all aspects of life, and diving is no exception. Despite the authoritarian teachings of certification agencies, there *is* a world below this imaginary boundary, and it beckons to be explored.

This then is Beyond Sportdiving—and the subject of this book. It is the forbidden world known only to those few who dare to venture into it and to challenge the limits of the envelope; it is a fantastic and surreal world seen only by a few of mankind's most adventurous. For the deep ocean floor is littered with the remains of some of man's greatest machines, broken and strewn about in a bewildering state of disarray, many never before seen by the eyes of man.

Diving does indeed become more complicated, and more danger-ous, at greater depths. The ambient pressure on a diver's body builds rapidly with increasing depth, at a rate of 1 atmosphere for each 33 feet of sea water. This steadily increasing pressure is the cause of most of the dangers facing the deep diver. Decompression becomes a serious concern: a diver must ascend slowly, stopping at predeter-mined intervals to allow nitrogen, which has been absorbed by his body's tissues at depth, to equalize with the decreasing pressure of the shallower water. To omit this decompression, to ascend too rapidly after a long or deep dive would bring about an attack of the bends, when nitrogen bubbles form in the joints, in the blood vessels, and even in nervous tissue. Expanding as the diver rises into a world of decreased pressure to which he has not yet adapted, the bubbles can cause excruciating pain, paralysis, and even death. Thus there can be no quick retreat to the surface if all does not go as planned. The dive must be carefully planned and air conserved to allow for this gradual ascent.

Nitrogen in the air we breathe (contrary to popular belief, the air in scuba cylinders is just that—plain, ordinary air and not oxygen) begins to act like a narcotic below a depth of approximately 100 feet. A popular analogy often taught in basic scuba courses is that of "Martini's rule." As the explanation goes, each 50 feet of depth beyond 100 feet is like one dry martini. Diving to 200 feet, therefore, is the equivalent of drinking two martinis. Although this is a simplification, it gets the idea across. Go too deep and a diver's motor functions and judgment become impaired; deeper still and he can become a danger to both himself and others.

Due to the increased ambient pressure on the diver's body, air is consumed more rapidly at deeper depths. The deeper a diver goes, the smaller his air supply effectively becomes. Bottom time must be curtailed, yet the narcotic effect of nitrogen at these depths requires more concentration and often more time to complete simple tasks. The result can be a vicious circle leading to a diver's ultimate nightmare—running out of air far from the safety of the surface.

This is very advanced diving, well beyond the scope of what is taught in basic scuba courses. The skills and knowledge necessary to make this type of diving a reasonably safe proposition come only through years of experience. The individuals involved in this extension of the sport are truly the best of the best, the elite of their world. And even still it is not without risk, for a few of the best, as well as a few less talented individuals, have lost their lives in the pursuit of their obsession. But the risks are known and accepted by those who choose to venture forth and explore this unknown world, and they dive with safety first and foremost in their minds. Although inherently more dangerous than shallower diving, these dives *can* be made safely.

With all the aforementioned risks and dangers, one is compelled to ask "Why?" Why risk one's very existence to explore the sunken hulks lost by generations past? Perhaps an unanswerable question, but an old one. Why did Columbus sail forth into an uncharted ocean in search of new lands many believed did not exist? Why did men brave inhuman conditions in a race to reach a theoretical spot in the frozen wasteland over the earth's northern pole? Why, indeed, did he spend billions in order that a very few could walk upon the surface of the earth's only moon? History is replete with such quests, as man has never stopped in his attempts to reach out into the unknown, to see and explore and conquer all that surrounds him. Our thirst for knowledge and exploration is insatiable, and it is this trait alone that truly sets us apart from the other inhabitants of this planet.

And so it is with diving. It is quite simply the exploration of a fantastic world unseen by land-bound men. For a few of us, this world has become the driving force in our lives, the focus of our every waking minute as well as our dreams, and indeed the very reason for our existence. It is not a sport—it is a way of life. This is the world that I would like to share with you.

Deep-Diving

Pioneers

As the sport of scuba diving began its slow but steady growth during the 1950s, the exploration of the many sunken ships littering the bottom of the coastal shoreline was a natural occurrence. The newly available Aqua-lung provided the means to satisfy the adventurous longings of the ordinary man on the street—for a deep-sea diver poking around the remains of a sunken ship is a common fantasy in almost every boy's childhood. Here was the opportunity to resurrect such dreams and bring them to life. The evolution of the "Jersey Wreck Divers" is a fascinating tale of the "iron men" involved in the infancy of diving along the U.S. East Coast.

The New Jersey and Long Island coasts have been the site of countless maritime disasters since men and their ships first sailed there from the Old World. The first recorded shipwreck in the region was that of Adriaen Block's ship *Tiger* in 1614, which caught fire and burned to the waterline while anchored in New York Harbor. New York was destined to become the busiest shipping port in the world, and the approaches to its harbor would claim an enormous toll in accidents due to the sheer volume of traffic alone. Collisions, acts of God and wartime hostilities would all claim their share. The density of shipwrecks here is rivaled in the New World only by the "Graveyard of the Atlantic" off Cape Hatteras to the south. A chart of all the known wreck sites off the northeast coast resembles a shot pattern, fired directly at New York Harbor.

Yet the exact location of most of these shipwrecks was unknown until quite recently. For many years these wrecks were merely vague references in history books and foggy thoughts in the minds of dreaming men. The story of diving the wrecks follows closely behind that of fishing them—for it was the fishermen who originally located the majority of wrecks known today.

In the early days, as it still is today, party boat fishing was a highly competitive business. Men were making their living by taking people out for hire to catch fish; those who consistently brought home more fish attracted return business, while those whose customers returned empty-handed didn't survive long. Any edge a captain could gain over his rivals put more bread on his table. Wreck sites provided just that edge. Just as a natural reef forms a home for an enormous variety and quantity of marine life, so does a shipwreck. Fishermen were quick to capitalize on this fact, and they began fishing the wrecks because they regularly produced fish. Wreck locations were closely guarded secrets since a fisherman's livelihood was dependent upon his ability to produce more fish than his neighbor.

At first, there were only a handful of known wrecks. Lying close to shore, they could be found consistently using land ranges by a good boat captain. While the offshore waters had been explored, returning to a wreck far from any point of visual reference was difficult. Although loran A had been available since the end of World War II, very few boat captains could afford to own the expensive receivers necessary to use the system. Necessity being the mother of invention, the old-timers developed a method to enable them to return to offshore wrecks that they had discovered. These old boat captains were masters at steering a compass course. They would leave an inlet and steer a known course for the one-mile buoy. As they passed the buoy, they noted their course error and corrected for the set and drift they had encountered on the way to the buoy. They would then set an ordinary kitchen timer for the required time and steer as exact a compass course toward the wreck as was humanly possible. They knew from previous journeys that the *Mohawk,* for instance, lay 40 minutes from the inlet on such and such a course. When the timer went off, they immediately threw a buoy over the side to mark the spot. Working a pattern around the buoy, they would search for the telltale wreckage on their bottom recorders. When the bottom topography was sloping or irregular, they would utilize its clues to help zero in on the wreck. Steering a compass course from the inlet for a set time, a good captain could usually get within about one-half mile of the wreck site. But a half-mile is a long distance on a featureless expanse of ocean, and it would often take several hours to find a wreck once the buoy had been thrown.

Later, as loran A became more readily available, more and more boats were equipped with this electronic aid. But loran A wasn't as sophisticated as its modern successor, loran C—in fact, it was notoriously inaccurate. Loran A was also difficult to use, and no two operators read the instrument the same way. Viewing an oscilloscope through a hooded port, an operator had to tediously turn a set of dials, trying to match up two sine-wave patterns. Once the patterns were matched, the numbers on the adjustment dials indicated the loran line. This was a demanding operation on a rolling boat, and it yielded only one loran line—the entire procedure had to be repeated to obtain a reading for the second line and fix the boat's position.

Despite the difficulties involved in finding offshore wrecks, the old-time boat captains were masters at it. They were constantly searching for new sites and their wreck books were closely guarded possessions. They spent their time fishing the wrecks and most were quite happy to return home with a good haul of fish and a boat load of happy customers. There were a few, however, who wondered just what was down there, on the bottom, in the fishes' domain.

The legendary Jay Porter, king of the wreckmen, was a man who wondered just what he was fishing on. Perhaps it was his curiosity that convinced him to allow a handful of divers to come out on some of his offshore fishing trips in the early 1960s. "Porter was one of the few captains who wasn't afraid of divers," says Captain George Hoffman, "although he thought we were crazy." Captain Porter would often travel hours, running far offshore to distant wrecks with a boatload of fishermen. As soon as a customer snagged the wreck with his fishing line, Porter would command, "Make way for the divers!" With that order, the handful of divers on board would scramble to get their gear together and jump over the boat's gunwale. Swimming over to the poor fisherman's snagged line, they would grab hold of the thin strand of monofilament and slide down, following it to the wreck below.

Porter ran the boat *Jess-Lu* out of Freeport, New York, for years, and was well equipped to find and fish the wrecks upon which his business depended. He was one of the few captains who had *two* loran sets on his boat, as well as sonar. Captain Porter discovered many of the wrecks we fish and dive today, and he is credited with naming such popular fishing sites, among others, as the "Virginia" and "Bacardi" wrecks (both of which are explored in more detail in later chapters of this book). Of course, Porter wasn't the only boat captain who took divers out to the wrecks. Other boats such as the *Albatross* run by John Schukis and the *Sea Ranger* run by Joe Galluccio also catered to divers, as well the *Comet*, run by Max Bendix, which was the first dive boat on the East Coast.

One of the first organized groups of wreck divers along the East Coast, the Ocean Historical Research Society (OHRS), was formed in the late 1950s. This group of early explorers deserves credit for the identification of many of the wrecks found in local waters. They were a small group, as interested in the history of the ships they dove as they were in the adventure of exploring the ships' remains. As this small organization slowly faded away, a few of the group's members formed the core for another, less organized, but no less adventurous clique of divers. This group bore no special name, but had in common an insatiable lust for diving and adventure. It was these pioneering wreck divers who would become, in the early 1960s, the first generation of deep divers along the East Coast.

By necessity, these early divers did most of their diving in the spring, fall, and winter months; summer was the fishing season, and the boats along the coast were too busy to be bothered with divers. But these men were obsessed by the hidden history they had found lying on the bottom of the ocean, and not even weather, cold, or hardship would keep them from that which they loved. Talking to Captain George Hoffman, who was one of these pioneering divers, and who still runs a boat and dives today, we hear tales of divers climbing back on board the boat by looping their arms through the rungs of the ladder, because the ladder was too thickly encrusted with ice to grab with their hands! He proudly exemplifies the spirit of these explorers with his stories of diving out of Montauk, New York, on Saturday, hopping into a car upon arriving back at the dock, and driving all night for a dive out of Cape May, New Jersey, the next day—and stopping for air fills along the way!

In those days there was no distinction between "deep" diving and "sportdiving"; diving was diving, and no one had placed any limits on how deep you could safely dive. Common sense prevailed; divers dove to the limits of their abilities, and no further. But they were not timid, either—these were hard-core divers, tough as nails and willing

The masts of the Brazilian freighter Ayuruoca *rise high above her decks, forming an impressive backdrop for photographers on rare days of exceptional visibility. Photo by Mike deCamp.*

to dive anything. The standard line to an inquiring boat captain on a rough day was, "If you can hook it, we can dive it!"—and they meant it, too! They dove anything they could get to; wrecks like the

Coimbra, "Virginia," "Bacardi," *Bidevind, Texas Tower,* and the "Oil Wreck" provided adventure for the taking. Each wreck provided an exciting new experience; no divers had ever visited these wrecks before. These divers were truly exploring the unknown, with unseen dangers lurking around every corner, and they loved every second of it.

They often worked hard and long trying to learn the identity of the sunken ships they dove. Such is the case with the large and mysterious freighter sitting upright on the western bank of the "mudhole" off the New Jersey coast, known then only as the "Oil Wreck." Sitting in 165 feet of dark and often turbid water, she was, and still is, intact but cleanly separated just aft of her bridge superstructure. Large and impressive, her identity was then unknown—but the divers were determined to learn her secrets. They sought vainly to recover some object from her that would reveal her identity.

While concentrating on exploring the ship's bridge section, believing it held the best chance of holding an identifiable object, George Hoffman plucked a ship's clock from the silt-laden interior one day. At that very moment, his dive buddy Mike deCamp anxiously waved his dive light at George through the darkened interior. Before Mike stood an old-fashioned, wooden desk—herein must certainly lie some clue to the identity of this mysterious vessel! George immediately dropped the clock he had found, and he and Mike struggled to carry the heavy desk out of the wreck. Unable to swim with it, they doffed their fins and carried the desk through the narrow corridors of the ship like two moving men in an ordinary house. After laboriously hauling their prize outside the ship, they quickly tied a lifting bag to it and sent it speedily toward the surface. The two divers then tied off their decompression reel and made their way slowly upward. Worried that they had sent the bag up untethered, George nervously broke his decompression just long enough to stick his head above water and shout to those already on the boat, "Don't let it get away, its got the secret of the 'Oil Wreck' in it!"

Surfacing nearly an hour later after a long hang, George and Mike clambered back on board, half expecting to be congratulated; they felt certain the desk must hold the answer to the elusive puzzle of the

"Oil Wreck." But strangely, silence and nonchalance reigned on board.

"Is it on the boat?" asked George, somewhat bewildered.

"It's on the bow," answered someone, indifferently.

Traipsing up to the forward end of the boat, they found the object of their endeavors sitting lamely on deck. As they approached, they noticed an unpleasant odor emanating from the desk.

As the two divers pulled down the front cover, they quickly discovered the reason for the lack of enthusiasm displayed toward their find (as well as the source of the foul smell)—their "desk" turned out to be an old-fashioned water closet!

Later, John Dudas brought up the clock that George had dropped in favor of the "desk." Its engraving showed that it had been built by the Chelsea Clock Works, and it had a serial number on it. The clock company was able to trace the number in their records and determine that it had been sold to the Lloyd Brasileiro shipping line for the Brazilian freighter *Ayuruoca*. This bit of hard evidence confirmed Mike deCamp's suspicions. He had run across an entry in the *New York Times* for June 12, 1945, reporting a collision between the SS *General Fleischer* and the *Ayuruoca*, and the subsequent sinking of the Brazilian vessel. Suspecting that this might be the vessel the group had been diving, he had ordered several photographic enlargements of the ship's bridge area from the Mariners' Museum in Newport News, Virginia. He had taken the photographs down with him on a dive to the bridge; comparing the two, he found that they matched perfectly. The serial number on the clock was icing on the cake—the wreck now had a name!

On another, rather productive day of diving on what they now knew was the wreck of the *Ayuruoca*, George Hoffman recovered the engine telegraph from the ship's bridge, while John Dudas swam up the ship's forward mast to the crow's nest and claimed her large bronze bell, which had fallen there as neatly as a ball in a bucket.

Although these adventurous weekend divers had explored many wrecks, visiting the remains of countless unknown ships and often reidentifying them for the world, there was a constant, nagging call that they would eventually be compelled to answer: What of the

On one productive day of diving on the "Oil Wreck" both the ship's bell and bridge telegraph were recovered. From left to right: Mike deCamp, George Hoffman (who brought up the telegraph), Walt Krumbeck, John Dudas (who recovered the bell), and Bill Hoodiman. Photo courtesy of George Hoffman.

diver's Everest, the *Andrea Doria*? The calling to dive the most famous of modern shipwrecks reached its climax during the winter of 1966; they would arrange a charter for the coming summer.

Once again, the team of George Hoffman and Mike deCamp swung into action, taking a dream and turning it into reality. The pair chartered Captain Paul Forsburg's *Viking Starlite* for the trip, and scheduled the expedition for the coming June. Captain Forsburg was a fishing-boat captain; he had never been to the *Doria* and relished the opportunity to fish this essentially virgin wreck for codfish. The two organizers had to scratch around a bit to find a handful of divers they felt were competent to dive this challenging wreck, but after scouring the East Coast they managed to come up with eleven willing and able souls.

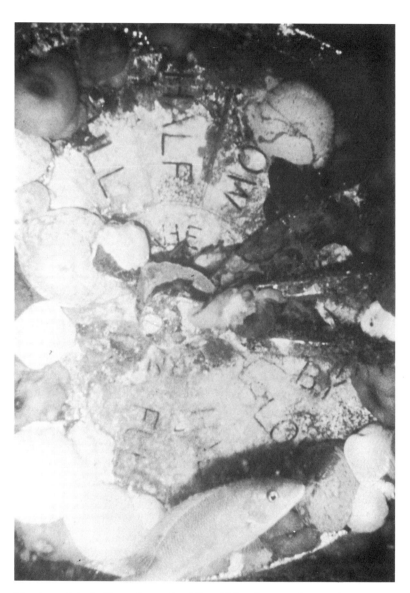

The face of the bridge telegraph while still in place on the wreck. The telegraph was found hanging by its chain over the side of the ship's bridge. Photo by George Hoffman.

Unfortunately for the anxious adventurers, hurricane Alma sprung up in the Caribbean just ten days before their scheduled departure. Sure enough, when time came to leave Montauk, New York, the early hurricane was making its way up the East Coast just in time to make things rather unpleasant on the open ocean. Not knowing what the seas were like offshore, or just what course the approaching hurricane would take, the divers elected to dive a new and mysterious wreck for which Forsburg had recently obtained loran numbers. Braving heavy winds and rough seas, the *Viking Starlite* managed to find and anchor into the wreck. The boat captain had done his job and located the wreck in the heavy seas; now it was time for the divers to perform. Descending the anchor line through the turbulent ocean, the divers found an intact submarine resting upright on the sandy bottom under 160 feet of water. Just what sub this was would remain a mystery for some time yet, although one individual managed to recover the ship's helm from within the open conning tower. But the divers were treated to perhaps one of the most amazing sights ever witnessed underwater. Reaching the top of her hull at 135 feet, they were astonished to find the entire submarine bouncing gently up and down under the influence of the huge ocean swell running above! To this day, according to George Hoffman, "Mike (deCamp) and I still joke that if we had put a 500-pound bag on her, we might have brought up the whole sub!"

Almost six months later, the profound cause of her most unusual bouncing act on the bottom of the ocean was discovered. In December, diver Bill Hoodiman, who earlier had measured the stem on one of the submarine's hatch dogs, used a wrench he had custom-made to undog one of the tightly closed entrances into the ship's interior. But the intervening years in the deep and corrosive ocean between the unknown time of her demise and the present had taken their toll on the steel structure; the hatch remained stubbornly stuck closed. Running out of bottom time, Hoodiman was forced to return to the surface. Unbeknownst to the clever diver, however, there was a powerful force from within the wreck trying to open the very same hatch. As Mike deCamp and George Hoffman passed Bill Hoodiman on their way down to the wreck, a tremendous and deafening roar suddenly filled their ears. Reaching the conning tower, they made their way cautiously aft, toward the source of the resounding rumble. Out of the hazy, deepwater gloom emerged a sight that George says he will carry with him to the grave: out of the now sprung-open hatch, a 48-inch solid column of air was blasting violently toward the surface!

Bewildered by the bizarre sight, the two curious divers swam cautiously toward the pillar of escaping gas. There they remained, watching, mesmerized with awe at a sight perhaps never seen before or since. But the supply of compressed air within the submarine was not limitless, and as it approached its end, sea water had to replace the evacuated volume of the submarine's hull. Just as a gallon jug of water turned upside down alternately spews water and sucks in air in a glub-glub-glub fashion, so the submarine began to do the same. As the open hatch alternately expelled air and sucked in sea water, it was all the two, now-frightened divers could do to hold on and avoid being drawn into the maelstrom that was quickly filling the vessel's interior. Fortunately, the submarine filled with water before the divers ran out of air. The air trapped inside her had provided enough buoyancy to allow the submarine to bounce and gyrate with the swells of hurricane Alma months earlier. Who knows how far the submarine might have drifted in her lightened condition since the time of her sinking.

Anxious to explore the now-flooded interior, the divers took time off from work several days later to return to the sub. Entering the gloomy and cramped submarine through the narrow hatchway, Mike deCamp and George Hoffman once again led the way. White paint still glistened on the walls and fixtures. She had been dry inside for all these years! A short distance inside, they found what they were seeking. A normally insignificant crate, containing an electrical armature, bore the name "USS BASS" stenciled in black letters. The identity of yet another sunken wreck had been discovered!

The crew of the expedition to the Italian liner **Andrea Doria** *on board the* **Viking Starlite** *in 1967. From left to right: (back row) Calvin Preater, Jack Brewer, Frank West, Jack Brown, Dick Hilsinger and Evelyn Bartram Dudas; (front row) William "Smokey" Roberts, Ed Rush, Mike deCamp, John Dudas, George Hoffman holding the bridge compass, and Walter "Doc" Krumbeck. Photo courtesy of George Hoffman.*

The divers did, of course, manage to make it to the *Andrea Doria* after their initial dive on the *Bass,* although they first had to weather the passage of hurricane Alma in the relative safety of Block Island. The seas were rough and the fishing boat was ill-suited for three days at sea with 11 divers on board. There were no bunks, and the divers simply threw sleeping bags down on the hard deck; everything on board got soaking wet from the ocean swells constantly breaking over the boat's side. The spirit of adventure that highlighted this trip was perhaps best exemplified by George's response to an inquiry as to what treasures the divers had returned with: "We came back with ourselves!" he proudly declared.

The following year brought both better weather and wiser divers for a return trip to the great lady. After first obtaining permission from the boat's captain, the divers loaded a pile of lumber on board before once again departing from the safety of Lake Montauk, New York. George Hoffman made good use of the long trip out to the wreck by turning the load of lumber into a fine set of bunks, one for everyone on board; there would be no sleeping on the hard, wet deck for the divers this year!

The previous year they had anchored into the stern bridge wing of the huge wreck, near the stern winter garden. In 1967, however, they had the good fortune of snagging near the navigation bridge, which was still in place at that time. Immense schools of pollack swarmed over the wreck's exterior as the divers explored the interior of the ship's bridge. It was here that John Dudas rescued the vessel's compass from the sea's cold embrace, saving it from falling to the sandy bottom far below when the entire bridge fell away several years later.

After their second visit to the famed Italian liner, this loose group of deep divers slowly began to dissipate. The vagaries of life slowly took their toll on the group; the individual divers drifted apart, each following his own calling. Many of them kept diving and remained in touch, but the cohesiveness that had made them the force of East Coast wreck diving disappeared.

But the wrecks themselves were still there, and it wasn't long before another group began to explore the deeper of them. The beginnings of this, the second generation of deep divers, found its roots in an organization known as the Manta Ray Diving Club. They would later form what was perhaps the most famous of the East

Coast wreck-diving groups, the Eastern Divers Association (EDA), which came into existence around 1971. This group continued to grow steadily until its peak in 1976, and then quickly dissolved, perhaps the result of growing too large.

During their reign over deep wreck diving off the New Jersey coast, however, these divers continued their predecessors' work. They were explorers, diving deep wrecks as well as those in shallow waters, researching their histories and attempting to identify unknown wrecks. Tom Roach, one of the driving forces in the organization, published many articles in *Skin Diver Magazine* about the group's adventures and discoveries.

Perhaps one of their proudest accomplishments was the identification of the two mysterious freighters sitting in the deep, dark depths of the New York "Mudhole." The two wrecks were known only by the odd names given to them by fishermen: the "Junior" and the "Greek." The two wrecks lie only one and one-half miles apart, and both are intact and sitting upright. Research had indicated that two freighters fitting their general description had gone down in this same area during World War II: the Greek freighter *Ioannis P. Goulandris* and the Chilean vessel *Choapa* (see Chapter 5 for the full story of their sinkings). The divers were fairly certain that these were the ships they had been diving on, but which was which? In fact, the name "Greek," which branded one of the wrecks, was a nickname for the *Goulandris*, spurred by fishermen's inability to remember the unusual Greek name. But this identification of the wreck was premature, and it turned out that the "Greek" was actually the *Choapa!*

Both of the wrecks were deep, lying in 200 feet of dark but often clear water. Bottom time was limited due to the depth, and determining which of the ships was which was a challenging task. Two methods of identification were contemplated. Enlargements were made of various distinguishing features of each ship from available photographs, so that the divers could compare these to what they saw underwater. Meanwhile, another team of divers would attempt to recover the helm stand and wheel from the bridge of the "Junior," where it had been spotted on an earlier dive, in the hope that it would bear some identifying legend. The former method had been successfully used by Mike deCamp to help identify the "Oil Wreck" as the Brazilian freighter *Ayuruoca* years earlier, while the latter method posed its own unique challenges at the depth in which the wreck lay.

On a cold day in late winter, the hardy divers left Brielle, New Jersey, on board Captain George Hoffman's dive boat *Sea Lion,* and headed to the wreck known then only as the "Junior." Arriving at the wreck site after a one and one-half hour ride, Captain Hoffman explored the wreck with the long sonic fingers of his fathometer, attempting to locate the ship's bridge, atop which stood the helm stand that all hoped would finally solve the mystery of the "Junior." After anxious minutes of probing, Captain Hoffman finally dropped a marker buoy on what he believed was the bridge superstructure.

As the first team of divers, Tom Roach and Gary Gentile, descended the buoy line, daylight faded first into twilight and then to night as the darkness of the mudhole engulfed them. Finally reaching the ship's main deck at a depth of 175 feet, it became obvious that they were not on the bridge. Just where on the ship's deck they had dropped was unknown, but a quick decision was necessary due to the great depth and its associated limited bottom time. Picking a direction, they began to swim along the ship's gunwale. After traveling more than 100 feet along a railing, they finally noticed the gunwale gently curving upward—they had reached the superstructure at last! Swimming to the top of the bridge, they came upon the helm for which they had come so far.

Quickly getting to work, the two divers began the tedious job of unbolting the helm stand from the deck. Struggling against both time and nitrogen narcosis, they finally got the last of the large brass nuts free using large pipe wrenches. Rocking the heavy helm stand back and forth, the two divers found that it was loose but would not come free. Dropping to the deck to examine the attachments again, they quickly discovered the source of the trouble: a large, 2-inch-diameter brass shaft was holding the stand in place—the drive shaft connecting the helm to the ship's rudder!

With no recourse left, they tied off their decompression line directly to the helm and began their ascent. After completing their lengthy decompression, they discouragedly boarded the *Sea Lion.*

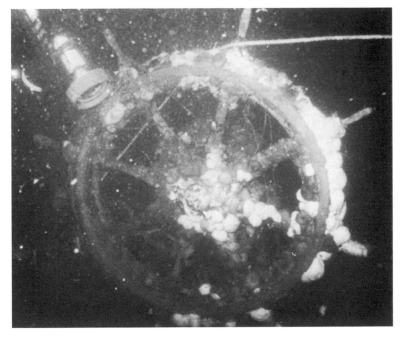

The helm and helm stand of the Ioannis P. Goulandris *served to help identify the wreck after it was brought to the surface by the members of the Eastern Divers Association. Photo by Mike deCamp.*

Back on board, they discussed the dive with their compatriots. The other divers had been more successful in their missions. Don Nitsch and Jan Nagrowski, after swimming to the vessel's stern, had discovered a huge double helm wheel perched upon the ship's poop deck, above a counter stern—these details matched perfectly with the photographs of the *Ioannis P. Goulandris* they had enlarged! For all intents and purposes, the mystery had been solved.

But the members of the Eastern Divers Association would not be satisfied until they had brought up some concrete proof of the ship's identity, and that meant the recovery of the bridge helm. The next two divers to enter the water, Bill Hoodiman and Bob Archambault, took a large bow saw with them to cut the 2-inch brass shaft that anchored the prized helm stand. Bill Hoodiman began sawing through the shaft while Bob Archambault took a closer look at what was holding the helm stand down. Here he discovered four more bolts that the other divers had missed. But the nuts of these last bolts were underneath the deck and inaccessible from above. Dropping over the side of the bridge while Hoodiman continued his assault on the drive shaft, Archambault entered the room below and began searching the ceiling for the elusive nuts. Incredibly, in the midst of the dark and silty interior, he found and managed to remove all four of the nuts. When he returned topside, Hoodiman had just finished sawing through the heavy shaft. The two began rocking the stand back and forth, just as the previous team had done. This time, however, the helm stand yielded and fell over onto the deck. The prize was nearly theirs, but their bottom time had expired! In their last few remaining seconds, the divers managed to tie on and inflate a lift bag before being forced to abandon the bottom and begin their ascent; but it was not enough to budge the heavy helm stand.

One last effort would be required to wrest the important object from the wreck's embrace. Tom Roach and Gary Gentile would have to return to the bottom on a short "bounce dive" to send the valuable artifact to the surface. Descending once again into the darkness below, the men reached the helm and quickly attached and inflated another lift bag, watching nervously as the bags and their cargo slowly ascended, picking up speed steadily as they disappeared from sight. The divers quickly followed.

After all had returned on board, and the prized and hard-won artifact was laboriously hoisted onto the deck of the *Sea Lion*, the divers anxiously began cleaning the stand, searching for clues to the ship's identity. On the stand's cap they found engraved the manufacturer's name, "Robert Roger & Co., Stockton on Tees." Here was the proof the divers sought; the *Goulandris* was built in 1910 as the *Eggesford* in Stockton, England. The pieces of the puzzle had finally fallen neatly into place. This left the "Greek" wreck as most likely being the sunken Chilean freighter *Choapa*.

Around 1977 EDA grew too large and disintegrated. With its demise, deep diving along the East Coast dwindled into obscurity.

To be sure, a few individuals continued to dive these challenging and compelling wrecks, but they were a rare and obscure breed. The wrecks lay largely dormant and undisturbed, and the occasional visit by curious divers was the exception rather than the rule.

Over the past decade, however, deep diving along this coast has again made a resurgence. Various small groups of divers are visiting these wrecks once again, as well as exploring a few new ones. The great Italian liner *Andrea Doria* has become an annual pilgrimage for many, and has even reached near tourist-attraction status, as adventurous divers from all over the country come to Long Island, New York, each July to try their hand at the old but still elegant lady.

We who now explore these wrecks, pushing beyond the established limits for sportdivers, are considered to be the third generation of deep divers. We dive many wrecks discovered and identified by our predecessors, as well as seek new discoveries of our own. And you can be sure that when we, the third generation, conclude our adventures, there will be fourth and fifth generations of deep explorers as well. Indeed, as long as there is water in the oceans, there will be men and women who will long to explore her depths. For there are always new and exciting mysteries awaiting those who are willing to venture into the unknown and explore the very limits of man's reach.

The
Identification
of the
Durley Chine

The
"Bacardi
Wreck"

———

———

———

———

———

———

———

———

———

———

Prologue

It is a damp, drizzly evening in late June 1987. Loading my dive gear aboard the charter boat *Seeker* in Brielle, New Jersey, I find myself thinking that the weather is exactly the same as it was for last year's charter to the wreck of the Norwegian motor vessel *Bidevind*. That trip also had a damp, dreary beginning and was followed by two days of rainy, rough weather in which our scheduled four dives had been cut to two due to high winds and rough seas. Would this year's trip follow the same pattern?

This year's charter was planned as a visit to an unidentified, almost virgin wreck called the "Bacardi Wreck," located a mere seven miles from the *Bidevind,* yet some 65 miles offshore. The legend of the wreck's name had been handed down through local, word-of-mouth folklore. The story has it that the legendary Captain J. Porter was running an offshore charter and had stumbled across a new wreck on which his passengers spent the day fishing. The fishing turned out to be so good that everyone agreed they must return to the same spot the following day. Captain Porter marked the spot with a weighted Bacardi rum bottle, donated by one of the passengers, so that he could find the wreck again. Ever since, the wreck has been known as the "Bacardi Wreck." Although the authenticity of this account is unconfirmed, the wreck has borne this name for as long as anyone can remember.

As far as we knew, the wreck had been explored only a few times by a handful of divers. Although it was popularly believed to be a barge, and thus of little interest to divers, two members of the Atlantic Wreck Divers Club, Jeff Pagano and Rick Jaszyn, had done a short "bounce dive" on the wreck several years earlier and dis-agreed. They had seen several portholes during their brief visit and felt that the wreck had potential. In fact, it was at their insistence that this year's trip, originally billed as a charter to the *Bidevind,* was diverted to the "Bacardi." Interestingly, Rick would later play the key role in the wreck's identification.

As the evening wore on, divers came on board, singly and in pairs; by ten o'clock, all 12 had arrived. Since the trip offshore would take about six hours, we were scheduled to leave at 3 A.M. After stowing their gear, most of the divers retired early, though a few of the guys wandered up the street to the Harbor Inn, a local gin mill, for a nightcap to mark their last night ashore. All were back on board by 5 A.M., when we finally departed after a few minor delays.

We arrived at the wreck site at eleven o'clock that morning. The "Bacardi" proved easy to find since the loran numbers had been common knowledge to fishermen for years. On the fathometer, the wreck appeared as a low debris field with several larger pieces rising 20 to 30 feet off the surrounding bottom. After dropping a buoy to mark the spot (a plastic antifreeze jug—there was no rum bottle available), the grapnel was let loose, and the wreck was snagged without difficulty. "Wreck fever" was running high that day, as it always does at the prospect of diving a new wreck. The divers on this charter were all experienced veterans, thirsty for some of the artifacts that they hoped might be lying among the broken bones of the vessel below. Little did they know just how productive this trip would be.

Diving the "Bacardi"

———

The back deck of the boat begins to buzz with activity as the crew of the *Seeker* gears up to go down and set the hook. Everyone else on board readies their gear and makes last minute equipment checks. Lights are tested and decompression schedules written on underwater slates. Blasts of air can be heard as divers ensure that their regulators are working properly and that their tanks are topped off. The wreck is deep and the divers want to be sure that they have plenty of air.

"What's the bottom read?" someone asks, referring to the depth reading on the ship's fathometer.

"Looks like about 180 or 190," someone replies.

The two mates roll over the side to set the anchor, but find they need help reaching the bow of the boat due to the strong current. Someone quickly throws them a length of line before they are swept aft, past the stern of the boat and beyond reach. Using the line, the divers are towed to the bow of the dive boat where they grasp the anchor line and begin pulling themselves to the bottom.

The seas are moderate and only a 2- to 4-foot chop mars the ocean's surface. The skies slowly begin to brighten as the cloudy, dreary weather starts moving out. As the minutes tick by, everyone on board anxiously scans the water, looking for a floating styrofoam cup, the standard signal from the divers below that the anchor is securely fastened to the wreck and all is well. Finally the cry of "Cup's up!" is heard, and everyone scrambles to don their gear and get in the water.

A "geriatric line" is rigged from the stern to the bow so that the divers can pull themselves forward to the anchor line, rather than swim against the strong current. Rick and Jeff hit the water first— they were almost fully dressed when the mates entered the water. Competition is often fierce to be the first in the water, especially on lobster wrecks, in order to get the best shot at whatever lies below. At times this eagerness extracts a large price, however; if there is any problem finding or grappling the wreck, the fully dressed diver must endure the hot, baking sun in a heavy one-quarter inch neoprene dry suit and full gear until the task is accomplished. But today there is no wait and the sounds of divers entering the water can be heard in rapid succession from all sides of the boat. My dive buddy on this trip is Gene Howley and we both agree to take our time and wait for some of the confused activity on the deck to clear before getting ready for our dive.

After the deck clears a bit, we finish donning our gear and check our air supply for the 14th time. I can't help but wonder what awaits us on the bottom, a distant 180 feet below. What kind of wreck is this? Is it merely one of countless sunken barges littering the bottom of the

Atlantic as is popularly believed? If so, this dive will be a waste of time, better spent on some more productive, known wreck than in search of some elusive, virgin site. What unknown hazards lie before us? The wreck may be covered with fishing nets billowing overhead, lost by commercial trawlers and waiting to trap an unwary diver. Since the wreck is frequented by fishermen, there is certain to be a heavy layer of monofilament enshrouding every available snag. The webs of tangled monofilament pose a serious hazard to the diver, who often becomes entangled in them. Several sharp knives are a must on all wreck dives.

"How are you doing, Gene?" I ask.

"Just about ready."

"OK, I'll see you on the bottom. Twenty minutes, right?"

"Sounds good to me."

These will be the last words spoken between us for the next hour. I get up and stagger across the pitching deck to the boat's gunwale. Balancing myself on the rail for an instant, I roll off the boat into the choppy sea. The current is indeed strong and I almost miss the geriatric line, just managing to grasp it with my outstretched hand and avoid being swept behind the boat. Pulling myself hand over hand to the bow, I revel in the crystal clear water found this far offshore. The northern coastal waters are not known for their clarity and many people refuse to dive here. Most prefer the clear, warm waters of Florida and the Caribbean. But travel far enough offshore and the change in the water is astounding. The dark, green, murky waters familiar to the beach-bound diver change to a clear, indigo blue that instantly captures the heart.

Reaching a depth of 10 feet, I stop briefly to start the timer on my dive watch. Struggling down the line, I find the current strong, but it begins to abate at a depth of about 50 feet. Continuing downward, we pass divers on their way up to their first decompression stop at 30 feet. We flash the universal OK sign at each other and continue, the water darkening with increasing depth. At 120 feet my eyes strain downward, looking for some sign of the wreck. I see none. We descend farther still and my eyesight begins to close in with tunnel vision, one of the first signs of nitrogen narcosis. We reach a depth of

160 feet and still there is no sign of wreckage, only a smooth, sandy bottom. Momentarily puzzled, I redirect my eyes forward, suddenly realizing my error. I have been looking straight down, but the anchor line has been given a lot of scope because of the strong current and there is nothing directly below me. Now looking straight ahead, I catch my first glimpse of the "Bacardi Wreck." It is sprawled out on the sandy bottom like a deepwater junkyard, its form at first unrecognizable. Settling to the bottom, we check our gauges and begin looking around, trying hard to fight off the numbing nitrogen narcosis. Recognizable forms begin to take shape before our eyes, like some giant jigsaw puzzle finally coming together after careful study.

The anchor line, stretching in a long, gentle curve leading back to the surface, meets the wreck at the old vessel's propeller shaft, where it has been securely tied by the crew of the *Seeker*. Stretching beyond our vision, the shaft fades gradually into the clear but dark water. The shaft is still supported by the struts and bearings that once held it in place while it drove this small vessel, although the rest of the ship has long ago collapsed around it. Large, hoop-like frames surround the shaft at uniform intervals—all that is left of the shaft alley that once enshrouded it. While broken and twisted hull plates lie strewn about in jumbled disorder on either side, the propeller shaft lends a sense of order to the debris as it runs straight and true down the center of the wreck. Off to the right, two large boilers loom out of the haze, cloaked in the bottom gloom much as the surface fog enshrouded the dive boat some hours before. I turn and begin swimming to my left toward a large, shadowy shape just visible in the distance. Passing over scattered rubble that was once a stout and seaworthy ship, I begin to recognize the stern section of a small ship, intact and lying on her port side, listing toward the sand. The propeller shaft ends abruptly just short of this after section.

Swimming around the stern and over what was once the deck, I see the remains of the steering quadrant jutting upward at an angle, poised on the end of the rudder shaft as if awaiting its final command. In the twisted shambles below me, a round, metal object catches my eye. It appears to be a bowl of some sort, and my first instinct is to pick it up and deposit it in my mesh bag. In my enthusiasm I imagine it is the compass bowl from the ship's binnacle. Later, back on board the *Seeker*, I am disappointed to find that it is the remains of an ancient lamp, horribly corroded almost beyond recognition. Adding insult to injury, Jeff Pagano sneaks over to tell me that he had picked it up on his dive, only to toss it aside as a piece of junk! We have a good laugh about it before throwing it overboard.

Probing further behind the stern to the very end of the wreck, I find the rudder intact, extending below the steering quadrant and disappearing into the sand, its lower end completely buried. Just forward of the rudder, one blade of a large propeller protrudes menacingly from the sand; beyond the prop blade, the keel of the vessel runs forward until finally blending into the sand in perfect camouflage. The lines of the hull viewed from astern are still striking, even in the ship's present state of decay on the ocean bottom, where she is surely embarrassed to be seen.

Glancing at my air gauge and bottom timer, I see that I have been wandering about the bones of this ancient vessel for fifteen minutes—leaving only 5 minutes to meet up with Gene, regain the anchor line and begin our ascent. As I head forward, following the propeller shaft like a road map, I glance back for one last glimpse of the stern. Lying on her side like a sadly stricken animal, this small ship, while lacking the impressive majesty of more famous wrecks such as the *Andrea Doria*, is still beautiful in her own way, lying quietly on the bottom in this incredibly clear water. As I reach the anchor line where Gene is waiting, I spot two small cargo winches lying upright in the sand and make a mental note of them. These indicate that the ship was probably a small freighter.

We begin our return to the surface reluctantly. Rising up the anchor line, hand over hand, we find ourselves looking back to savor every last glimpse of the wreck. Such is the frustration of wreck diving, never being able to spend enough time on the bottom, always cursing your finite air supply and the limits imposed by decompression. Perhaps this frustration is what makes this sport so obsessive. There is always the desire to return, to see what was unseen or only glimpsed on the last dive, to explore every last corner of every last wreck, because it is unknown and calls out to you and demands your return.

Sliding slowly upward at the 60-foot-per-minute ascent rate demanded by the decompression tables, we dread the boring but necessary thirty minutes of "hanging" that separates us from the safety of the surface. This can seem interminable when hanging on to the anchor line for dear life in a strong current, or when overcome by the chill-induced urge to urinate caused by more than an hour's submergence in the icy North Atlantic. Today is no exception and the minutes tick by excruciatingly slowly as our arms begin to ache from clinging to the anchor line, fighting the current's efforts to pull us away from the line's security.

Finally it is time to surface. Struggling against the current to reach the ladder hanging off the transom, we climb back on board the dive boat where we can finally relax again. As each of the divers return from their dives, there is much discussion as we all attempt to piece together a picture of the wreck from the multitude of individual accounts. Most have seen the two large boilers amidships, indicating that our mystery ship was a steam-powered vessel. It soon becomes apparent that about half of the divers have visited the stern of the vessel, while the other half have seen the ship's bow section.

Since I had seen only the stern, I am most interested in hearing what the bow section looks like. The reports are impressive. Rick Jaszyn had been to the bow and told us that it was intact and pointing upright, much like a teepee. He said that it looked just like the bow of the "Virginia Wreck," another deep, East Coast wreck familiar to the handful of hardy divers on board. According to Rick, however, this vessel had a bowsprit extending from its prow. We had already established that she was a single-screw, steel-hulled steam vessel—but with a bowsprit? Although no masts had been sighted, the bowsprit indicates that the ship must have been rigged as a sailing vessel as well. This was quite common on early steamships since their engines were considered too unreliable to provide the sole source of power for an ocean-going vessel. The bowsprit could prove to be an important clue in establishing her age. It was also apparent that she was a fairly small ship—collectively we had quite easily covered the wreck from stem to stern in a single 20-minute dive. From Rick's description, the bow sounds as if it must be quite impressive and I decide that I must see it for myself on the next dive.

The time on the surface between dives is spent napping, eating, talking, and fiddling with dive gear. Some compared notes on different parts of the wreck, while others laid plans for the next dive. But to all on board, this time spent on the surface between dives is but a necessary evil, passed restlessly while awaiting the next dive.

A surface interval is required between any two deep dives, and it is part of the decompression schedule spelled out by the U.S. Navy Standard Air Decompression Tables, as well as any other decompression method presently available, such as the decompression meters that have become increasingly popular in recent years. If a diver were to return immediately to the bottom after completing his first dive, his body tissues would contain so much dissolved nitrogen that he would only be able to stay on the bottom for a very short period of time before the required decompression stops became entirely prohibitive. By spending time on the surface at atmospheric pressure, the amount of nitrogen in the body is slowly reduced to a level where a second dive of practical length becomes possible. The necessary surface interval for dives at this depth ranges from about three to six hours, depending on the length of the two dives and how much time the diver is willing to spend "hanging" on his second dive.

When enough time has finally passed, the divers begin preparing for their second dive of the day. Some have plans to work on a project they started on their first dive, while others just want to poke around for any loose artifacts they might find. Portholes and china are always popular among divers, and on a virgin wreck such as this, there is always the possibility of finding one of the real prizes of wreck diving, such as the ship's bell or helm stand.

I have decided to visit the bow section on my second dive. In clear waters such as these where visibility is commonly in excess of 40 feet, just gazing at the unnatural beauty of the wreck can be awe-inspiring in itself. As I enter the water, my intention is to see for myself as much of the wreck as possible and to photograph it (with, of course, one eye always peering around the next corner for any stray artifacts!).

Rolling over the port gunwale of the *Seeker,* we must once again fight a strong current on our trip to the anchor line, but it is an expected obstacle this time and so it seems less bothersome. Reaching the ocean floor after our long descent, we go through the familiar ritual of checking gauges and turning on dive lights before leaving the anchor line. As I part with Gene and begin my swim toward the bow of the decaying ship, I feel a deep uneasiness wrenching at the pit of my stomach. It is a lonely feeling swimming about a ship's skeleton beneath the ocean, accompanied only by the native fish and an occasional lobster. At such great depths, a solitary diver is far from help. He must be totally self-reliant and prepared to deal with any circumstance that might arise. This fear and loneliness is compounded by the effects of nitrogen narcosis gnawing at my brain. The uncertain feeling of parting with the anchor line, the only sure link with the surface world from which we came, and the fear of the unknown that lies ahead is both frightening and exhilarating—like some fantastic and exciting surreal dream.

Leaving the anchor line, I swim ahead to the end of the massive propeller shaft, which ends in the skeletal framework of a collapsed steam engine. The silhouettes of the ship's two large boilers loom overhead. They sit side by side, perched upon a bed of crumpled beams and hull plates. Three furnace doors can be seen in the lower face of each boiler, peering out like huge eyes at all who dare to pass through this unearthly place. Swimming farther forward, I focus on a massive shadow beginning to take shape in the deep gloom before me. I pass over more cargo winches and much unidentifiable wreckage before I finally recognize the shadow ahead.

What stands before me is a truly spectacular sight. Sitting on a bed of clean, white sand stands the prow of this once-proud, little steamship. Intact and pointing skyward, the prow rises above the ocean floor like some magnificent cathedral. Protruding vertically from its very peak is what looks like a long bowsprit. Its form is hazily masked by a tight winding of nets lost by some poor fisherman long

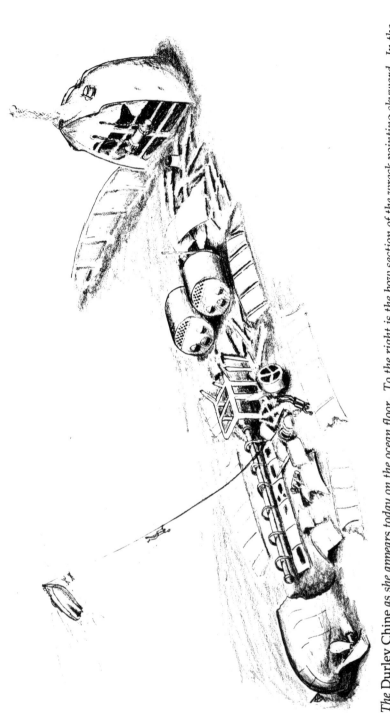

The Durley Chine as she appears today on the ocean floor. To the right is the bow section of the wreck pointing skyward. In the center lie the two boilers and the collapsed steam engine. The propeller shaft extends towards the stern, which lists to port. Drawing by author.

ago, unsuspecting of what lie below. The prow is flanked by two large navy anchors, one on either side, each one protruding from its respective hawsepipe. The chains are still in place and lead up through the deck and around a large windlass before disappearing into the bowels of the bow. All that remains of her forepeak deck are the slender deck beams—the deck plating has disintegrated, long ago rusted to rubble by the destructive ocean. A solitary porthole peers out at me from the fo'c'sle—a silent reminder that men once inhabited this tiny, broken vessel.

Swimming vertically up the deck to the very tip of the bow, I stop to examine the anchors, now shrouded in abandoned fishing nets. Upon closer examination of the ship's bowsprit, I see that it is but a shadowy mirage, consisting merely of a twisted mass of nets, held aloft and pointed upward by the round floats that once held the top of the net afloat. There is no bowsprit on the ship after all.

Looking down the ship's stem toward the vessel's bottom, I can see clear evidence of a collision with some unyielding object. Though the hull plates appear intact and unbroken, the stem itself is grotesquely twisted, and there appears to be an obvious indentation where the vessel hit something hard. More clues to her identity perhaps? This is unmistakable evidence of a head-on collision—yet the hull plates behind the apparent impact point appear unbreached. Perhaps the impact buckled the entire hull some distance back from the bow, crumpling the forward section and separating it from the rest of the hull. Such a scenario might also explain why the bow sits in its peculiar attitude on the bottom, pointing skyward.

Once again my bottom time has passed too quickly, and it is time to begin the lengthy swim back to the now-distant anchor line. I swim backward at first, intent on absorbing the incredible scene laid out before me. I find myself longing to stay and explore further but am compelled to leave by the limitations of my human physiology. Again I pass the huge boilers, the broken engine, and all the intervening wreckage until I finally arrive back at the anchor line, my guide to the more hospitable world above.

After completing our lengthy decompression, we return to the incessantly rocking world aboard the *Seeker* for the evening. Dinner is a mishmash of cooked and uncooked foods, with everyone on board contributing something to the potpourri. There are cooking facilities available, including a microwave, but some still prefer the ease of cold cuts and sandwiches three times a day. Stories are told and books read for the remainder of the evening until, one by one, everyone crawls off to some corner of the cabin to curl up for the night. Sleep comes easily—the boat's motion is gentle, and everyone is tired from a long day of diving.

The Discovery

———

Dawn comes early, bringing with it a bright, sunny day with a crisp breeze blowing out of the southwest. Two more dives are made today and with them comes the discovery of the ship's identity.

On his first dive of the day, Rick Jaszyn finds himself poking around the wreckage just forward of the ship's boilers. He is looking for nothing in particular, just scrapping for anything he might come across. Peering under the right hull plate from just the right angle, he spies a curved edge of bronze protruding from the hard, white sand. His heart pounding, Rick digs frantically, for he immediately recog-

The bell recovered on June 28, 1987, by Rick Jaszyn, which identified the long mysterious "Bacardi Wreck" as the Canadian steamship Durley Chine. *Photo by author.*

nizes the object. It is buried securely, but he finally manages to free the cast-bronze ship's bell with only seconds to spare before his bottom time runs out. With barely enough time remaining to tie it to a lift bag, he quickly inflates the bag and sends his trophy to the surface.

The identity of this long-forgotten shipwreck is still a mystery to Rick as he anxiously completes his decompression. The suspense is

Rick Jaszyn proudly displays his well-earned prize from the deep. Photo by author.

almost more than poor Rick can bear. Some sixth sense from within makes it plain to him that he is the focus of an important moment in history.

For those on board the *Seeker,* the mysterious identity of the "Bacardi Wreck" has been uncovered. A diver is sent out to retrieve the lift bag as it breaks the surface. Little does anyone suspect the significance of this simple act. While the throb that goes through our collective hearts upon seeing the elegant little bell lifted clear of the ocean and set on the deck of the dive boat can't be compared with Rick's thrill at finding it, the moment is nevertheless magical.

While Rick fights the strong current below, impatiently anticipating his return to the surface, all on board revel at his discovery. For inscribed in bold letters, laboriously carved into the bronze bell, is the legend:

SS DURLEY CHINE
1913
CARDIFF

Epilogue

―――

Rick was beside himself when he finally climbed back on board the dive boat. Everyone there felt the intense excitement of the discovery, along with the thrill of being involved in the identification of the wreck. But the moment was Rick's, and the expression of pride echoed by his impish grin as he clambered up the boat's ladder will live long in the memories of all who were there to see it.

He was justifiably proud of his find. A ship's bell is the most highly sought-after artifact of any wreck diver, and most divers will never be lucky enough to find one. Not only did Rick recover the ship's bell, he had solved a long-standing mystery to both divers and fishermen alike: the identity of the "Bacardi Wreck."

Although her name is now known to the world, the history and circumstances behind the demise of the steamship *Durley Chine* have proved somewhat elusive. To date, no photograph of the vessel has been located, and only after much research have the details of her sinking come to light. Perhaps this difficulty is testimony to the seeming insignificance such a small coastal vessel plays in the grand scheme of things. Her sinking went unnoticed by the world at large, save a short paragraph appearing in the casualties column of the *New York Maritime Register* on April 25, 1917. Only a lawsuit between the two ships involved in the accident has left a trace of the details.

The *Durley Chine* was built in 1913 by Osbourne, Grahm & Co. of Sunderland, England, for the Alum Chine Steam Ship Company. While originally registered in 1913 in Cardiff, a major shipping port in Wales, she was later registered to the port of Ottawa, Canada, in 1914. At this time she was owned and operated by the Canadian government.

A rather small, coastal cargo vessel, the *Durley Chine* measured only 279 feet in length with a 40-foot beam. According to her registration document, she had two masts, a small open forecastle and poop, and a long center island bridge. She was registered as being 1157 net tons, and her small 209 net horse power triple-expansion steam engine was capable of driving her at a speed of only 9.5 knots. According to *Lloyd's Register,* her master was D. R. Davies.

The SS *Durley Chine* met her fate while on a voyage from Halifax, Nova Scotia, to Norfolk, Virginia, in ballast. She was to pick up a load of coal in the U.S. port, but she would never reach her destination. At 1:19 A.M. on April 22, 1917, she collided with the British freight steamer *Harlem*, which was outbound from New York and heading for Bordeaux, France, with a cargo of munitions. Here the *Durley Chine* sank, approximately 65 miles southeast of the Ambrose Channel Lightship. Her captain and entire crew of 28 seamen were picked up by the *Harlem*, whose own bow was bent and leaking from the impact. The *Harlem* returned to port with the rescued crew of the Canadian freighter, and was forced to undergo repairs in dry dock.

On the dark night of April 22, 1917, the British freight steamer Harlem *rammed and sank the Canadian steamship* Durley Chine. *A lawsuit between the two vessels placed the blame for the collision on the Canadian vessel. Drawing by author.*

The cause of the collision was a matter of controversy and lawsuits were filed by the owners of both vessels, each claiming that the other was at fault. The detailed circumstances of the collision are preserved in the court proceedings between the two vessels.

The accident occurred on a dark but starlit night with a slight haze hanging low over the horizon. The *Durley Chine* was headed approximately southwest (S 50° W) and traveling at a speed of about 9 knots. The *Harlem* was traveling southeastward (S 52° E) at a speed of 7.25 knots. The vessels were traveling at almost exactly right angles to one another, with the *Harlem* off the *Durley Chine*'s starboard bow, thus having the right-of-way as spelled out in "Rules to Prevent Collision at Sea."

Such a situation would seem to place the blame for the collision clearly on the captain of the *Durley Chine*. But the master of the Canadian vessel claimed that the *Harlem* was at fault, and the owners of the *Durley Chine* were, in fact, the plaintiffs in the ensuing lawsuit. According to Captain Davies' account, his vessel was traveling southwestward, sounding the fog signals appropriate for the hazy conditions. While the lights of the *Harlem* were seen several minutes prior to the collision, the captain and second officer of the *Durley Chine* claimed that the other vessel was displaying only a dim, white light (the masthead light) and no sidelights. Unable to ascertain the heading of the approaching vessel, the *Durley Chine*'s captain stopped and reversed his engines while throwing the helm hard-a-port to counteract the effect of his ship's right-handed propeller. Not until the *Harlem* was nearly alongside could her course be determined by the commander of the *Durley Chine*, who, at that point, was able to see the hull of the other vessel in the dim light. The two vessels were apparently parallel to one another and would have cleared each other but for the subsequent actions of the British steamer. By now the reversal of the engines aboard the *Durley Chine* had brought her to a near standstill in the water. No sooner did the Canadians see the hull of the oncoming vessel than the *Harlem* changed course to port and bore down upon the doomed ship, cutting so deeply into the *Durley Chine* that the crew was forced to abandon her in short order. She stayed afloat for several hours, however, before finally disappearing at about 5 or 5:30 in the morning.

The master of the *Harlem* disputed the statements of the plaintiff, claiming that his vessel was indeed displaying the proper navigation lights. Furthermore, since the *Harlem* had the right-of-way, he kept her on course until it became obvious that the other vessel would not yield and a collision was imminent. At that time, the helm of the

Harlem was put hard-a-port and her engines were ordered full speed astern in order to avoid the other vessel.

The master of the *Durley Chine* did not contest the fact that the other ship had the right-of-way, but only claimed that he could not tell because the *Harlem* was not displaying sidelights. Thus the court proceedings amounted to the question of whether or not the *Harlem* was displaying the proper navigation lights. As the two accounts differed in regard to this critical question, the court concluded that the statements of "one or other of them must be knowingly false." The court decided in favor of the *Harlem* and Justice J. Drysdale stated in his judgment: "I find that the *Harlem* before and at the time of the collision was carrying proper regulation lights. I believe the officer of the *Harlem* in this connection. I think the *Durley Chine* solely to blame for the collision." Not satisfied with this judgment, the owners of the *Durley Chine* appealed to the Supreme Court, but the case was dismissed.

One mystery remains unsolved by the existing accounts, however. The crumpled and leaking bow of the *Harlem,* along with the court testimonies, indicate that the bow of the British vessel hit the Canadian ship and caused her to sink. Yet the bow of the *Durley Chine* wreck shows clear evidence that she collided head-on with some unyielding object. Is this an indication that the vessel was involved in another collision prior to the one that proved fatal and the damage left unrepaired? Or is it possible that the two ships collided nearly head-on, despite the accounts given by the two crews? The position of the ship's bow section, pointing upward from the sea floor indicates that this damage could not have occurred when the ship hit the ocean bottom.

With the discovery of the ship's bell, a long-unanswered riddle has been solved. The identity of the small steamship *Durley Chine,* undisturbed on the ocean floor for 70 years and known only as a good fishing snag called the "Bacardi," is now certain.

Is This the

Sommerstad?

———

———

———

———

———

———

———

———

———

———

———

———

———

———

———

———

The "Virginia Wreck"

───────

Far out to sea, some 40 miles southeast of Fire Island, New York, and beneath 170 feet of clear, blue water lie the remains of a large steel freighter. Known locally as the "Virginia Wreck," her real identity is shrouded in mystery. Local legend has it that she was named by an Italian customer of charter boat Captain Jay Porter who mistook the fact that they were fishing a "virgin" wreck for the name of the sunken ship under them, and she was thereafter called the "Virginia." Her fishing virginity having long ago passed into oblivion, she is now one of the most popular offshore fishing sites to be found south of Long Island. During the busy summer season, local newspaper fishing columns often quote the captains of successful fishing charters as having been "out near the Virginia Wreck."

Although her location is well known to any offshore fisherman worth his salt, her grave site is not marked on any government navigation charts. Indeed, her very existence seems to have gone unnoticed by the authorities. Located approximately halfway between Fire Island Inlet and the Hudson Canyon, she sits as a lonely sentinel to the approaches of New York Harbor. In an area of the eastern seaboard littered with the remains of sunken ships, she rests in solitude with no other known wrecks within a 15-mile radius. Thus she appears as a glaring omission from National Oceanic and Atmospheric Administration (NOAA) charts dense with wreck symbols and obstructions.

Though frequented by offshore fishermen nearly year-round, most divers shy away from her remains. A kind of superstitious phobia has grown among divers toward this wreck over the years due to two tragedies that occurred exactly one year apart. Twice divers have lost their lives on the wreck, and their memory hopefully serves to remind both the experienced and inexperienced alike of the dangers involved in deep diving.

Her appearance on the bottom is a scene of total confusion, the midships section a chaotic jumble of twisted steel hull plates and broken beams. Amid the debris can be found a few familiar forms, however. Two large boilers, one of which is upended, are situated halfway between the bow and the stern. The steam engine appears to be missing or reduced to unrecognizable rubble. Forward of this lies a spare propeller standing on end, and there are numerous small windlasses lying about.

The bow provides a strong contrast to the scattered wreckage stretching astern. Whole and unbroken, it points nearly skyward, leaving a diver with the impression that the old hulk has not yet accepted its fate on the bottom of the ocean and is still trying to regain her rightful place on the surface. Similarly, the extreme stern remains fairly intact, listing on its starboard side. Running forward from the after-section lies a long propeller shaft, seemingly searching for the

The ship's propeller shaft stretches neatly along the center of the wreck, surrounded by a network of frames much like that on the Durley Chine. *Photo by author.*

missing engine that once drove it. Running straight and true, surrounded by the frames that once formed the shaft alley deep in the bowels of the ship, it offers a sense of order to the surrounding wreckage. Fishermen scanning the wreck with a recorder generally pick up two high peaks surrounded by low-lying wreckage. These peaks represent the twin boilers and the slightly higher bow section.

She gives the appearance of being a very old wreck, battered for years by winter storms that have hastened her decay. Nevertheless, it is difficult to believe that natural forces alone are the cause of her extensive deterioration. It is a commonly held belief that she was depth-charged as a suspected submarine during World War II, although this is purely conjecture. This would account for the state of her remains, as well as provide an explanation for the condition of the portholes recovered from her by divers. Many of the portholes have been found severely bent and twisted, their glass apparently shattered and dispersed long ago.

Other than a few portholes, only two artifacts of any significance have been recovered from the wreck. The ship's helm, a battered, destroyer-type wheel, was brought up years ago. More recently, the vessel's engine telegraph was recovered. Neither of these two relics have provided any concrete evidence of the wreck's identity. The ship's bell presumably would provide positive identification, but it awaits discovery, hidden somewhere among the vessel's broken remains. Until the day when some lucky diver stumbles across this prize, we must attempt to identify her by the twisted trail of evidence she has left behind.

The *Sommerstad*

It is 8 A.M., August 12, 1918. World War I is in full swing, and the German Kriegsmarine has had a handful of submarine raiders operating off the American coast for almost three months now. These *unterseeboots,* as the Germans call them, have been making quite a nuisance of themselves, sinking steamships and sailing vessels alike by both torpedo and shellfire, laying mines in harbor entrances, and even harassing the fishing fleets on the Georges Bank.

A light, early morning fog hangs low over a calm ocean south of the Long Island coastline. The 340-foot-long Norwegian steamship

The 340-foot-long steamship Sommerstad *was built in 1906 at Newcastle, England. She was sunk by the German submarine U-117 on August 12, 1918. Photo courtesy of The Peabody Museum, Salem, Mass.*

The large "U-Cruiser" U-117 survived the war and was transferred to the United States. She was brought back to the East Coast for study and use in the "Victory Bond" campaign. Photo courtesy of National Archives.

Sommerstad is making a slow but steady 11 knots westward toward New York Harbor under the command of Captain George Hansen. There she will pick up vital cargo to return to the war effort in Europe. Wireless messages were picked up the day before warning of U-boat activities off the American coast, but the reports placed the submarines some 200 miles away, and Captain Hansen does not expect them to be operating this close to the Long Island coast.

Unknown to Captain Hansen, another vessel lurks nearby. Hidden from sight beneath the peaceful surface of the ocean, Kapitan-Leutnant Droescher of the German Kriegsmarine silently guides his large submarine *U-117* toward a fateful meeting with the Norwegian steamship. Having just completed the long Atlantic crossing from Germany to their destination off the coast of America, the crew of the submarine is anxious for action. While *U-117* is primarily a mine layer, she is also carrying 12 torpedoes and is equipped with 2 deck guns, providing her with ample firepower to wreak havoc with merchant shipping. And that is just what her commander has in mind. Taking full advantage of his unknown presence, Kapitan-Leutnant Droescher conducts a submerged attack on the unsuspecting freighter, using only his periscope to close in on his prey.

Captain Hansen joins his first and second officers on the bridge. While he feels they are too close to the coastline for submarines to be a threat, he is nevertheless nervous about their possible presence. Looking out over the calm ocean from the port bridge wing, Captain Hansen glimpses something out of the ordinary. He cannot make it out and so picks up the glasses, straining to identify the object to no avail. Several minutes pass and still Captain Hansen cannot make out the object.

Suddenly, out of the haze appears the wake of a torpedo traveling at high speed directly toward them off the port beam.

"Reverse engines! Full speed astern!" cries Captain Hansen.

Hansen and his officers stand transfixed, watching as the deadly torpedo speeds toward their ship at nearly 40 miles per hour, much too rapidly to alter the ship's course in time to avert disaster. But, incredibly, the torpedo passes harmlessly under the *Sommerstad*'s keel, just forward of the bridge, and the men let out a long sigh of relief.

But their relief is short-lived; watching the torpedo travel away from their vessel, they are astonished to see it turn to the left, come about 180 °, and pass the ship again, this time forward of the *Sommerstad's* bow.

"Full speed ahead!" orders Captain Hansen.

Astonishment quickly turns to horror, however, as the torpedo turns yet again, coming full circle, and heads back toward their ship for a third time. Unable to escape the relentless torpedo, the small ship is struck aft on the port side with a terrific explosion. Several men standing on deck are knocked down, and the cook is blown out of the galley by the force of the explosion.

Seeing that his ship will not last long, Captain Hansen orders his crew to lower the ship's two boats and leave the *Sommerstad.* The ship is hastily abandoned, with the 31 sailors escaping the sinking vessel with only the clothes on their back. Settling rapidly, her funnel is awash only four minutes after the torpedo strikes. She begins to sink by the stern, and as the sailors get the boats clear, her bow rises, pointing skyward in her last gasps at life. The *Sommerstad* soon disappears entirely from sight, leaving the sailors alone on a vast ocean in their two tiny boats.

The men set out toward the Long Island shore to the north. The sea is calm and they make good progress. Still it is near sundown some 11 hours later when the men are finally spotted by a naval patrol craft, shortly after hearing Fire Island's fog horn. The patrol boat takes them on board for the night, and carries them to the safety of New York Harbor the following day. The only injuries sustained throughout the entire ordeal were the sprained ankles of the captain and another sailor who jumped from the ship's deck into the life-boats.

One and the Same?

———

While the *Sommerstad* met a swift and sudden death, the German submarine *U-117* managed to survive the war after sinking several more vessels off the American coast. After hostilities ended, she was one of the 176 U-boats handed over to the Allies and eventually divided up between Britain, the United States, France, Italy, and Japan. The *U-117* was turned over to the United States, making an ironic return to the East Coast under the command of her former enemies. Here the vessel was not only dissected for technical study but was also used as an exhibit for the post-war Victory Bond drive.

The U-117 *was dissected and studied before being sunk off Cape Charles, Virginia by aerial bombardment on July 22, 1921. Here workmen gaze down into the intricate inner workings of the submarine's engine room. Photo courtesy of National Archives.*

She was finally relegated to her rightful place in the deep when she was sunk by aerial bombardment along with *U-140* and *U-148* on July 22, 1921, 50 miles east of Cape Charles, Virginia.

The SS *Sommerstad* has now lain beneath the surface of the North Atlantic for over 70 years. Having endured countless winter storms and a second World War taking place overhead, her hull surely must show the ravages of time. But where do her remains lie? A twisted and sometimes confusing trail of evidence has been left behind that, after careful research, lends credence to the theory that she and the "Virginia Wreck" may be one and the same.

Contemporary newspaper accounts place her "about twenty-five miles southeast by east of Fire Island . . ." This position is almost 20 miles north of the "Virginia Wreck" and is not a likely match. However, buried deep in the archives of the U.S. Department of the Navy is an obscure document entitled *Publication Number 1: German Submarine Activities on the Atlantic Coast of the United States and Canada*. Published in 1920, it presents a careful analysis of the U-boat operations off the American coast during World War I, based on the data available at the time, and contains details of the *U-117*'s sinking of the SS *Sommerstad*.

The location given for this fateful encounter is 40° 10' N latitude, 72° 45' W longitude, only six nautical miles from the true location of the "Virginia Wreck." This position is seemingly contradicted in the same report where she is placed "about 25 miles SE of Fire Island." This apparent contradiction can be resolved, however, by recalling that the Fire Island *Lightship* was then stationed some 15 miles south of the present Fire Island lighthouse. Taking "Fire Island" to mean the *Lightship* location causes the two given positions to coincide almost exactly. This interpretation also fits nicely with Captain Hansen's story of the lifeboat trip toward shore when he states, "Toward sundown we heard Fire Island's siren, and made directly for the shore. Soon afterward we were sighted by the naval patrol vessel which brought us to this city." On a slightly foggy evening, the *Lightship*'s foghorn would be sounding its steady, monotonous blasts like clockwork to warn ships off the Long Island shoreline to the north. It is also a more likely location for the naval vessel to have been on patrol, rather than close enough to the beach to be within range of the lighthouse's foghorn.

Other details provided by Captain Hansen in his report to the American officials fit quite well with the evidence available on the actual wreck site. The *Sommerstad* was bound for New York from Halifax in water ballast—she was carrying no cargo. There is no

This bridge telegraph was found and recovered by Sharon Kissling and Sally Wahrmann in 1987. The telegraph handle was stuck in the "Full-Speed-Ahead" position. Is this an echo of Captain Hansen's last order as he desperately tried to avoid the U-boat's torpedo? Photo by author.

evidence of any cargo on the "Virginia"; either there was none or it perished long ago. The telegraph recovered from the wreck was found half-buried in the sand beside the wreck, its handle long frozen in the full-speed-ahead position. Remember that Captain Hansen ordered full speed ahead just before the torpedo struck, desperately trying to avoid its third and final pass at the ship. Is the frozen handle of the telegraph recovered from the "Virginia" an echo from the past, reflecting Captain Hansen's last order? The face of the telegraph bears its manufacturer's name, based in Glasgow, Scotland. The *Sommerstad* was built in 1906 by R. Stephenson & Co., Ltd., Newcastle, England. The shipbuilder would have undoubtedly employed equipment and machinery from regional manufacturers in the construction of the vessel.

The "Virginia Wreck" lies along an approximately east-west axis, with the ship's prow at the westernmost end of the wreck. This orientation mimics the final course of the *Sommerstad* when she was torpedoed by the German U-boat. Her bow sits pointing skyward from the sea floor, much like an Indian tepee. This obviously did not result from the ship sinking bow first, but more likely from sinking by the stern, with the bow the last part of the vessel to leave the surface. Again, drawing on Captain Hansen's report, "The *Sommerstad* filled so quickly after the torpedo struck her that in four minutes she had settled so deeply that her funnel was awash. The steamship began to sink by the stern and as we got the boats clear her bow was pointing skyward."

Reminiscing about my first dive on the bow section of the "Virginia," I can easily picture this grisly scene based on the evidence laid out before me on the ocean bottom. Standing on the white sand bottom 170 feet below the surface, staring upward at the upended bow through the crystal-clear water, this nearly forgotten moment in time comes spilling forth from the annals of history. One can almost hear the shouts as the men scramble into the lifeboats, with Captain Hansen jumping from the ship's rail at the last instant, spraining his ankle in the process. It is truly a majestic sight, and one can easily be led to believe that this is indeed the remains of the Norwegian freighter *Sommerstad*.

At the very peak of the bow, the hull plating is holed and badly deterio-rated. Just below the gunwale is a small, round hawsehole which matches exactly with the one visible in the photograph of the Sommerstad. *Is the "Virginia Wreck" the Norwegian steamship* Sommerstad? *Photo by author.*

The *Sommerstad* was a steel-hulled steamship measuring 340 feet in length with a displacement of 3,875 tons. She was powered by a triple-expansion steam engine supplying 301 n.h.p. to her single screw. Her home port was Sandfjord, Norway, and she was owned by A. F. Klaveness & Co., although she was under charter to the United States government at the time of her sinking.

The "Virginia" is about the right size and age from all appearances to be this vessel. The wreck lies in the correct location and orientation on the bottom (heading west, toward New York). Indeed, it is the only known wreck in the vicinity of the *Sommerstad*'s sinking. The intact bow, pointing skyward as the *Sommerstad*'s was when she sank, is quite broad with a perfectly plumb stem, appearing identical to that of the Norwegian freighter. This is true down to the smallest detail seen in the only known photograph of the ship, including the round, ringed hawsehole near the very peak of her bow. The accompanying photographs of the wreck point out some of these features, which can also be seen in the photograph of the *Sommerstad.*

Examination of all available information presents a convincing argument that this wreck is indeed the same one torpedoed by the commander of *U-117* in August 1918. Just as important, the evidence produces no contradictions that would disprove the wreck's identity. Yet one nagging detail seems out of place. Since the U.S. government obviously knows the location of the *Sommerstad's* sinking (the U.S. Navy's *Publication Number 1* documents its location), why does it not appear on the NOAA chart? Almost all shipwrecks whose locations are known appear on these charts, and so it seems a strange omission. A chance discovery provides the explanation, as well as furnishing the final brush stroke for the picture painted here.

The National Oceanic and Atmospheric Administration maintains a computerized file of all wreck and obstruction information in its possession for use in preparing navigation charts and for planning future surveys. Dubbed AWOIS (Automated Wreck and Obstruction Information System), its files are available to the public for a small fee in the form of a computer listing. Paging through this hefty volume of material, I ran across an interesting entry:

No. 01498 SAMMERSTAD [sic]   40/08/00.00 073/53/ 00.00. . . CARGO, 3875 GT; SUNK 8/12/18 BY SUBMA- RINE; POS. ACCURACY 1-3 MILES REPORTED THROUGH CGS SURVEY, DATED 4/1/23 (REG. NO. NOT ASCERTAINED) SEE SOMMERSTAD

The actual position of the "Virginia Wreck," now well established in this day of accurate loran receivers, is (to the nearest minute of latitude and longitude) 40° 08' N, 72° 53' W, identical to that listed in the AWOIS printout except for the obvious transcription error in recording the longitude position of the wreck as 73° 53' W. Thus it would appear that a U.S. Coast and Geodetic Survey (CGS) correctly located the wreck of the *Sommerstad* on April 1, 1923, but, perhaps befitting the fact that it was All Fools' Day, incorrectly recorded her position. In keeping with this error, a wreck symbol appears on NOAA chart no. 12300 at 40° 08' N, 73° 53' W, only 6.5 miles off Sea Girt, New Jersey (note that one degree of longitude at this location is approximately equal to 45 nautical miles). By the simple mistaken stroke of a pen, a mysterious and long-standing riddle was unknowingly perpetrated.

Although some will undoubtedly still question the "Virginia's" identity, and perhaps correctly demand a more concrete and traditional identification of the wreck by the finding of her ship's bell, I know in my heart that she is indeed the torpedoed freighter, SS *Sommerstad*.

The

New York

"Mudhole":

Deep,

Dark,

and Dangerous

—

—

—

—

—

—

—

—

—

—

—

The "Mudhole"

Extending southward from New York Harbor, a mere ten miles off the New Jersey shoreline, lies a deep trench in the sea floor. This trench extends southward to a point just east of Asbury Park, where it turns and continues southeastward until it runs off the continental shelf and into the abyss of the deep ocean some 70 miles south of Long Island. The waters in this undersea valley are considerably deeper than those surrounding it. Off Asbury Park, where the ocean floor is an unintimidating 100 feet down, the depths of the "mudhole," as it is affectionately called by the locals, are twice that. The depth gradually increases to 250 feet to the southeast, until the valley extends past the continental shelf and drops into the deep ocean floor at depths of several thousand feet in an area known as the Hudson Canyon.

The Hudson Canyon, where the mudhole valley meets the edge of the continental shelf, was named for the river by which it was formed. Some 17,000 years ago, when much of North America was covered by a tremendous sheet of glacial ice and the surface of the sea was 300 feet below its present level, the continental shelf lay above water and formed the coastline of the North American continent. The mighty Hudson River flowed southward across the shelf to meet the sea, but the sea was 70 miles farther south than the present river mouth, now the location of New York Harbor. Fed by the enormous glacier, the Hudson then dwarfed its present-day remnant. The tremendous flow of water through the river, combined with the glacial movement of the ice itself, carved a deep river valley into the continent's bedrock. When the ice melted and the sea rose once again, this valley disappeared beneath the advancing ocean and became an undersea canyon. The original valley was carved to depths as great as 950 feet below modern-day sea level. Much of this has since been filled by sediments carried south by the Hudson for thousands of years, bringing the mudhole's depths to their present levels. These sediments, lying beneath the cold waters of the Atlantic, form a black, silty mud that fills the bottom of the trench and provides the origin of the name mudhole.

By no coincidence, the north- and south-bound shipping lanes leading into New York Harbor pass right over the mudhole. Ships sailing north toward New York Harbor are, in essence, traveling up the ancient but unseen extension of the Hudson River. The congested and often confused shipping traffic outside of New York Harbor during World War II provided the impetus for a number of collisions and subsequent sinkings in these waters. While the convoy system was relatively easy to operate in the vast expanse of the open ocean, it became unwieldy in the close confines of the approaches to harbors and ports. The chaos that resulted as both inbound and outbound convoys attempted to navigate the narrow channel forming the entrance to New York Harbor only added to the danger. As a result, the bones of more than one vessel lie in the dark, forbidding depths of the mudhole. The victims of such collisions must be added to the list of those vessels sunk directly by the German U-boats, which the convoy system was designed to overcome, as they are certainly casualties of the "Battle of the Atlantic."

The Sinkings

―――――

On the first of December, 1942, the Greek freighter *Ioannis P. Goulandris* was proceeding north in convoy, attempting to minimize the risk of submarine attack, which was responsible for a multitude of ship sinkings off the American coast during the previous year. But at 10:23 P.M., a request for immediate assistance was heard over the wireless: the *Goulandris* had collided with the Panamanian SS *Intrepido* and was taking on water. Her position was first reported as "off Ambrose Flashing White Buoy." Upon receiving the distress signal the Coast Guard dispatched the tugs *Mahoning* and *Navesink*, as well

The Ioannis P. Goulandris *was a 362-foot-long Greek freighter owned by the Goulandris brothers. Originally built as the* Eggesford *in Stockton, England in 1910, she was sunk about 11 miles east of Asbury Park, New Jersey, on December 1, 1942. Photo courtesy of The Mariners' Museum, Newport News, Virginia.*

as several motor lifeboats. The tugs searched Ambrose Channel, but returned to port unable to find either vessel. Later, the position of the sinking was corrected to 40° 15' N by 73° 45' W, about 11 miles east of Asbury Park. The tug *Mahoning* was ordered to the corrected position along with the salvage vessel *Accelerate.* Along the way, the tug *Joseph H. Moran* was intercepted and also directed to the scene of the collision. The *Mahoning* later reported, "One engine disabled, do not know when we will reach destination." Luckily, amid all this confusion, the entire 31-man crew of the *Goulandris* was rescued by the *Intrepido,* where they stood by and sadly watched as the masthead lights of the Greek vessel disappeared beneath the surface of the darkened Atlantic.

Slightly less than two years later, on September 21, 1944, in almost exactly the same location, two more collisions occurred with one of them proving fatal. At 3:27 in the afternoon, the British tanker *Voco,* outbound for Halifax, Nova Scotia, in convoy HXF 310 ran into the Chilean freighter *Choapa,* which was inbound for New York as part of convoy KN 338. The collision was reported as having occurred at

The Chilean freighter Choapa *was built in 1937 as the* Helga *for J. Lauritzen. Later she was sold to the Chilean government, who owned her at the time of her loss on September 21, 1944. Photo courtesy of The Mariners' Museum, Newport News, Virginia.*

The Brazilian freighter Ayuruoca *was sunk on June 10, 1945, after colliding with the SS* General Fleischer. *Originally built in Germany as the* Roland, *she measured 468 feet long and displaced 6,872 gross tons. Photo courtesy of U.S. Coast Guard.*

Buoy "F" in New York swept channel. Just 18 minutes later, and in the same vicinity, the U.S. cargo vessel *John P. Poe* and the British tanker *Empire Garrick,* both members of the outbound convoy HXF 310, ran into one another. Both the *Poe* and *Garrick* suffered enough damage to force them to return to New York.

Meanwhile, the *Choapa* was in much more serious condition. While the *Voco* suffered only slight damage to her forepeak, it was apparent to the crew of the small Chilean freighter that their vessel was doomed. The entire crew of 30 sailors abandoned ship and were picked up by the *Voco.* Two-and-one-half hours after the collision, at 5:55 P.M., the *Choapa* bid goodbye to her crew and headed for her new home at the bottom of the mudhole, some 200 feet below the surface. Her position was reported as 40° 16' 44" N by 73° 47' 27" W, a mere one and one-half miles from the final resting place of the Greek freighter *Ioannis P. Goulandris.* Since it might be a possible menace to navigation, the *Choapa* was temporarily buoyed.

Nine months later yet another outbound freighter became a victim of collision at sea. On the foggy night of June 10, 1945, the Brazilian SS *Ayuruoca* was sliced neatly in two by the Norwegian cargo vessel SS *General Fleischer.* All but one of her 66-man crew were rescued by the submarine chaser *SC-1057.* She settled to the bottom a mere half-hour after the collision.

At the Bottom of the Abyss

_____

Diving these wrecks in the bottom of the mudhole is a unique experience—even to divers who frequent the deeper wrecks of the East Coast. The water they lie in is often quite clear, yet even on the best of days, the visibility is limited. The great depth of the wrecks limits the penetration of sunlight, and what little light does reach the bottom is absorbed by the bed of fine, black silt deposited over eons by the flow of the mighty Hudson. The result is an eerie and eternal world of darkness, virtually void of ambient light. Without a dive light it would be nearly impossible to see at all. Even with the most powerful light available, it is much like being locked in a huge, darkened room with only a small penlight beam to pierce the engulfing darkness. This perpetual night seems to magnify many-fold the already disorientating effects of nitrogen narcosis. Compounding the diver's dilemma even further is the deep layer of silt literally filling the wreck and lying on every exposed surface. The slightest touch causes the black mire to billow up into enveloping clouds, reducing the visibility to absolute zero. Abandoned fishing nets and cobwebs of monofilament pose another hazard, providing a constant source of both annoyance and danger as they reach out to ensnare anything or anyone coming within their clutches. The wrecks of the *Goulandris, Choapa,* and *Ayuruoca* all sit nearly upright and intact on the bottom, an unusual and enticing feature that draws the experienced diver to visit their remains. Most wrecks this close to shore are largely broken up and scattered about the bottom, often resembling a pile of rubble more than a ship. But the depth of the mudhole has made it unnecessary for the government to demolish the wrecks as hazards to navigation, and has also served to protect them from the destructive power of a stormy ocean. Yet, the very fact that these wrecks are intact presents its own hidden danger.

Once a diver reaches the bottom and leaves the anchor line to explore the wreck, there is no guarantee that he will be able to return to make use of it for his ascent. For this reason, all divers carry an ascent line with them, to be utilized in the event that they cannot return to the anchor line. But once committed to using such a line, a diver must wonder what unseen dangers lie in the darkness over-head. Might an abandoned fishing net be floating above, billowing from an upright mast, unseen and waiting for an attempted ascent by an unknowing diver? Rick Jaszyn tells of a time when just such a nightmare befell him while diving the *Choapa.* Tying a lift bag to the end of his ascent line at the end of his dive, he had little time to worry about the unseen dangers overhead. Until, of course, he felt his lift bag bumping its way jerkily past some invisible obstacle above him—an obstacle that stood between him and the safety of the surface, 200 feet above. The major portion of both masts still stand upright on the deck of the *Choapa.* Draping downward from the peak of each mast is an umbrella of heavy lifting cables, once used to support the network of cargo booms that loaded and unloaded the vessel's freight. Now encrusted with marine growth, the cables lie hidden, stealthily obscured by the darkness of the mudhole's depths. With no time remaining to seek out the anchor line he now desperately wished he could find, Rick's luck held and his ascent line made it through the maze of cables to the surface. But such a brush with danger leaves a lasting impression, never to be forgotten.

The conditions in the mudhole are harsh and dangerous, but it is due to this uninviting environment that these wrecks remain largely unexplored, and therein lies their great allure. The wrecks represent unexplored territory; they have been touched by only a few human hands since the events leading to their demise some 40 years ago. No one person knows them in their entirety; only through our collective knowledge can we piece together an accurate picture of their condition on the sea floor.

Artifacts and souvenirs abound on the wrecks, a direct reflection of their unspoiled condition. While the majority of the shallower wrecks in the region have had their most highly prized artifacts removed by an earlier generation of divers, these deeper wrecks still may hold a ship's bell, helm, telegraph, or similar prize.

Here diving is indeed an exploration of the unknown, where one can truly go "where no man has gone before."

The Majestic *Ayuruoca*

———

Lying in 170 feet of water on the western bank of the mudhole, the "Oil Wreck," as the *Ayuruoca* is often called, is the shallowest of the trio of freighters. Mimicking her final course, her bow faces south and her stern points toward New York Harbor to the north. The collision with the *General Fleischer* left her in two pieces, yet each half is nearly perfect. Sliced symmetrically in two at her midpoint, she sits upright and defiant on the muddy bottom. The two halves are separated by about 60 feet, and a diver theoretically could swim from one half to the other, but visibility generally precludes such a venture.

At the after end of the bow section, her towering bridge rises to within 110 feet of the surface. The bridge structure is intact and stately, with its railings and stairways in place. A diver can wander around the companionways and up and down the various deck levels at ease, yet there is something strange here. Although whole, and at first glance seemingly undamaged, the superstructure is but an empty shell. In the early 1970s members of the Eastern Divers Association (EDA) concentrated on this section of the wreck and recovered many artifacts. Yet she still remains a pretty and stirring sight. Her railings are often covered with a fuzzy halo of colorful marine growth, fluttering in the current and lending the scene a touch of the surreal. Swimming through her intact companionways is a pleasant and welcome treat not often enjoyed by East Coast wreck divers, and one that is not soon forgotten.

Dropping down into the even darker area forward of the bridge, several trucks can be found lashed to the main deck. They seem oddly out of place here, condemned to remain forever silent in this eerie world far from their intended destination. Ahead lie open cargo holds, dark and forbidding to the explorer. The two forward masts stand erect and complete to the level of their crow's nests, as do the after two masts on the nearby stern section.

The stern section proves to be fascinating, if sometimes confusing. The cut where the poor ship was broken in two provides easy access to both the midship deckhouse and the ship's engine room. Much exploring remains to be done here and, as if to prove it, a stash of china was recently discovered. Decorated with a 22-karat gold-leaf floral pattern, it appears to have been part of a personal collection being transported back home by one of the crew. Along with the china various containers of colorful cosmetics were discovered, raising interesting questions about the nature of the freighter's crew.

The broad expanse of the ship's deck is broken by open cargo holds, winch machinery, the two soaring masts, and several tow trucks lashed in place. At the very stern stands a round gun platform supporting a 5-inch deck gun, a sight commonly seen on merchant

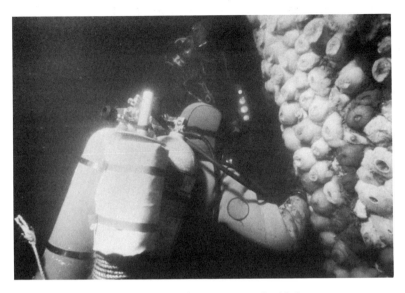

The exterior of the Brazilian freighter is carpeted with huge sea anemones, fed by the nutrient-rich outflow of the Hudson River. Photo by author.

vessels during the war. Underneath the gun platform, however, is a sight to behold. What at first appears to be a wall is soon recognized as a huge, auxiliary steering helm. Easily a full 7-feet in diameter, it stretches from deck to ceiling beneath the gun platform. So large is the wheel that my first glimpse of it left me dumbfounded: how was I to photograph this immense object? I had come to capture the wheel on film, but having never before seen it, I was at a loss as to how to proceed. My only recourse was to settle for photographs of part of the helm, for this was all that would fit in my camera's viewfinder. Stories abound of numerous divers trying to remove the enormous wheel, but to date none have been successful. The wheel remains for all who dare to venture forth to behold it, and for some as yet unnamed diver to someday claim it as his own.

First Encounter with the *Choapa*

"Rick, you see this grapnel?! It's never going to see land again!!!"

With that, George threw the cursed iron object overboard, and stomped off into the wheelhouse. This seemed to relieve his frustrations a bit, and he was finally able to snag the wreck below us with a more cooperative hook he produced from one of the *Sea Lion*'s storage lockers.

George Hoffman, captain of the *Sea Lion*, had been trying to snag the small bridge of the sunken freighter *Choapa* for a full two hours now, to no avail. A strange combination of wind and sea conditions

Exploring the Choapa's *bridge, the Atlantic Wreck Divers recovered much of the crew's china dinnerware, as well as her wooden helm wheel. From left to right: (back row) Steve Gatto, Dennis Kessler, Jeff Pagano (who brought up the helm and stand), and the author; (front row) Rick Jaszyn and Tom Packer. Photo by George Hoffman.*

today was making his work extremely difficult, and his frustration was beginning to show. He was attempting to drop the boat's anchor into the small bridge section of the freighter, a target only about twenty feet by thirty feet and lying 180 feet below the ocean's turbulent surface. His only tool was the sonic beam of a chart recorder which he used to "see" the wreck. This is a difficult task as evidenced by the fact that even George, one of the best in the business, was having difficulty today. The sea was rough, and the current was running down the length of the wreck; anything less than a perfect drop and the anchor would simply slide down the outside of the *Choapa's* hull without snagging on anything. It was important to the divers on board that he hook the bridge section—the highest part of the wreck, rising to a depth of only 170 feet. The mudhole is no place to go wandering about aimlessly, and the bridge section was where we expected to find the best artifact hunting.

It had been years since any serious diving had been done on the wreck, and we hoped to find her largely untouched. Some 20 years ago there had been a brief flurry of diving on the *Choapa*, and a few artifacts had been salvaged. George himself had brought up one of the ship's bridge telegraphs, and he never tired of proudly telling us that it was the most beautiful telegraph he had ever seen come off a local wreck, and George has seen plenty. In the intervening years, the small vessel lay virtually undisturbed, the deep depths and hostile conditions keeping away all but the most venturesome divers.

The rough weather, combined with the exceptionally long time that it took us to secure the *Sea Lion* to the wreck, only permitted us one dive that day, but it was enough to ignite what would quickly become an obsessive relationship with the small Chilean freighter. Rick Jaszyn and Jeff Pagano were the first team in the water, and secured the grapnel to the top of the ship's bridge. They then dropped inside and began working on two large, brass windows. It was the second group of divers, however, Tom Packer and Pete Guglieri, that made the major find that would seal our union with the wreck for years to come. Dropping down the front face of the small bridge, they stopped to peer into a small, corroded hole leading into the interior. Scattered amidst a deep layer of silt lay dozens of china dinner plates!

Barely able to squeeze through the tiny opening with their bulky dry suits and twin tanks, they managed to retrieve several dozen plates and returned with them to the surface. Dennis Kessler later brought up another bagful of china. All told, there was enough china on board so that everyone went home with a sampling of dinnerware from the old vessel. Examining the white plates, we found a small, blue flag emblazoned on the rim. Within the flag the mysterious four letters "CSAV" were inscribed. The meaning of these initials was quickly deciphered, however, as Tom and Pete had also recovered several wine glasses with a somewhat different emblem cut into the glass. Here the same flag was surrounded by the inscription

"COMPANIA SUD AMERICANA DE VAPORES," the shipping company that owned and operated the *Choapa*.

———

———

It is a calm, sunny morning in August 1987; nearly two years have passed since our first exploration of the *Choapa*. Today will mark our sixth visit to this deep and compelling wreck. Pete Guglieri and I discuss our dive plan on the way to the wreck site. We plan to work a small hole in the floor of a small "porch" running along the after side of the ship's bridge. This area has been productive on our past two trips, and we hope that our luck will continue.

Our dive plan calls for Pete to send up a decompression line directly outside the hole, while I venture inside and dig through the silt in search of china. This will save the time usually spent relocating the anchor line at the end of the dive, allowing us to spend more of our precious bottom time digging for our elusive quarry. Pete must also station himself at the hole leading into the dark interior, using his powerful dive light as a beacon to aid me in finding the exit once I disturb the thick layer of silt that has settled in the ship's interior. Without his light to aid me, I might become hopelessly lost inside until my limited air supply is exhausted, unable to find my way out. When penetrating most shipwrecks, the way out is marked by the dim, green glow of exterior light making its way into the wreck's interior through portholes, doorways and other openings. But there is no ambient light here; the exterior is just as dark and gloomy as the interior and we are forced to provide our own exit beacon.

Once the wreck is located, Captain Hoffman concentrates on zeroing in on the ship's bridge, which rises some distance above the main deck. Only after he is certain that he has properly identified the correct section of the wreck, the mate drops a buoy to mark the spot, and George grapples the wreck. When the grapnel snags home, he readies a second anchor line with two short lengths of sisal rope tied to the end in lieu of an anchor. The first team of divers has the responsibility of dragging this second line down to the bottom and tying it securely to the wreck as near as possible to the bridge. The second team of divers then follows the first line to the bottom and frees it, sending it to the surface with the help of a lift bag. This leaves the boat tethered to the wreck with one anchor line, secured with sisal rope.

When the diving is done for the day, George can use the boat's engine to break us free from the wreck, since the sisal is much weaker than the parent nylon line. This procedure avoids the need for a diver to descend and "pull the hook," manually freeing the anchor from the wreck as is normally done in wreck diving. George has developed this procedure exclusively for these deep mudhole wrecks, where a diver's bottom time is severely limited and too precious to be wasted freeing the anchor.

Rick and Jeff are in the process of suiting up since they will be the first team of divers today and tie us into the ship's bridge. Pete and I make up the second team, and will release the original grapnel line before continuing our dive. As Rick and Jeff go over the side of the boat, Pete and I begin preparing for our dive. The ocean surface is a flat, glassy calm, a sign of potentially good conditions on the bottom. Looking over the prow of the *Sea Lion*, we see the anchor line reaching down into the seemingly black water some 35 feet before fading from view. Visibility appears to be excellent. After a long 20 minutes, the escaping bubbles from the first team of divers can be seen preceding them up the anchor line as they return to the surface. Their dive is over except for the lengthy decompression they must complete; with both anchor lines now secured to the wreck, Pete and I complete preparations for our dive.

Making a final check of our gauges, we plunge over the side into the mirror-calm Atlantic. We find the water exceptionally clear, and can easily see the two anchor lines stretching downward from the *Sea Lion's* bow from our vantage point under her stern. Rick and Jeff hang calmly onto one of the lines, enjoying the crystal clear waters surrounding them as they decompress. Proceeding to the bow, we follow the first anchor line downward toward the mystery and adventure awaiting us.

The bright, clear waters of the surface quickly fade and give way to the crystal clear blackness that is the mudhole's realm. Engulfed in an eerie, infinite void, where our only reference is the narrow line we follow blindly downward, I begin to wonder why we are here. I must painfully acknowledge my mortality and take wonder at what fools we are to challenge this alien world. The darkness deepens, and then grows blacker still until I think it can get no darker, and yet it does. Finally we are forced to turn on our powerful dive lights to see the anchor line we are following, and to avoid a head-on collision with the wreck when we finally arrive. We must tread softly here; we are mere visitors in this dark, untamed underworld where mystery reigns and unexpected challenges to our very existence loom around every corner.

An unforeseen dilemma begins to confront us as we continue our long descent: the two anchor lines have started to diverge, apparently heading to vastly different parts of the stricken ship. When we finally reach the bottom, the second line, which was tied to the wreck by Rick and Jeff and is our only sure return to the surface, has long ago disappeared from our sight. We find ourselves amid a tumbled confusion of masts, cables, and cargo booms somewhere on the ship's deck—we don't know exactly where. Our developing fears have been confirmed; once we free our descent line and send it to the surface, we will be completely on our own, with only faint hope of being able to locate the remaining line securing the dive boat to the wreck.

Pete struggles to free the grapnel from a tangled maze of monofilament while I awkwardly fumble with a lift bag—nitrogen narcosis is always more noticeable during the first few moments of a deep dive, and today is no exception. Pete cuts the last few strands of monofilament entangling the grapnel with his razor-sharp knife, while I release a last burst of air bubbles into the lift bag. We both watch numbly as our only link with the surface drifts upward and out of sight, steadily accelerating as the air in the bag expands as it rises. As it disappears from view we glance at each other with questioning eyes as if to say, "What now?" while the full impact of the defiant act we have just completed strikes home. We are alone in an alien world, immersed beneath 200 feet of dark water, perched among a confused mass of wreckage that neither of us recognizes from our few previous visits. Somewhere in the darkness around us is a thin line that leads back to the safety of the surface above, but where?

A glance at my gauges tells me we have only fifteen minutes remaining before we must begin our ascent. Shining our lights over the surrounding carnage, it is not clear which course to take. I motion to Pete and point ahead in a direction chosen at random and we begin to swim, examining wreckage as we go. The scene unraveling before us makes little sense. We pass over what appear to be cargo booms and rigging lying in a jumbled heap upon the deck. This is a scary place, but the fear is thankfully numbed by the effects of high-pressure nitrogen. We wander slowly forward, attempting to avoid dangling masses of abandoned monofilament and hoping to find some recognizable piece of wreckage from which to gain our bearings.

Suddenly we run head-on into a wall of steel! Swimming upward, examining it as we go, we find a railing and then another wall several feet beyond the first. Incredibly, groping our way blindly along the deck of this lost freighter, we have come upon the stern side of the bridge superstructure at the exact spot we had planned on working! Simultaneously we both realize where we are and quickly get to work. Pete removes the decompression reel stored against the double tanks on my back. As he prepares our ascent line, I drop through the floor of the platform on which we are kneeling into the dark abyss below. Visibility is excellent inside; the interior is still undisturbed as I am the first diver to enter the "china room" today.

Descending to the deck, I shine my dive light slowly around the room's interior, taking in the strange panorama surrounding me. I am kneeling in a bed of fine, black silt perhaps a foot deep, but the dark muck shares the deck with hundreds upon hundreds of glass bottles. Everywhere I look wine bottles and beer bottles of all shapes and sizes litter the bottom of this small room. But bottles are not among the items we have come looking for today, and my eyes scan the area in search of a glimpse of exposed white china. After carefully

Deep inside the Choapa's *bridge lie hundreds upon hundreds of wine and beer bottles. Note the extensive accumulation of silt which fills the ship's interior. Photo by author.*

scrutinizing the deck around me, I find nothing of interest lying exposed and begin digging amongst the bottles, hoping that my hands can discern what is hidden from my eyes. Slowly and deliberately, I grope through the thick soup of black muck and bottles, carefully examining each object I encounter by feel until I can discern its identity. I work my way across the deck inch by inch for what seems like hours, although I know full well it is only minutes, and still I find nothing but bottles.

Frustrated, I begin to stuff dozens of bottles into my mesh bag, refusing to leave this dark hole empty-handed. I reach for my gauges and struggle to read their message in the murk I have created. The effort is to no avail—I cannot read them. Indeed I can barely see the glow of my dive light through the maelstrom of suspended sediment, even though it is only inches from my face!

Sensing intuitively that I still have a few minutes remaining, I move to my right a few feet, and begin digging in a new area, hoping that my luck will soon change. Pushing aside the myriad of bottles lying on the surface, I plunge my hands deep into the mud. At last I feel a flat, round object which I immediately recognize as a small plate. I deposit the plate in my goody-bag and begin frantically searching for more. I know that my time is nearly gone, and I must soon begin my return to the surface.

Suddenly I hear a garbled torrent of shouts from directly over-head. Pete is getting restless at his station at the hole's entrance; he also realizes that we must soon begin our ascent. Quickly I stick my mitted hand back into the silt and pull out a small wine glass. More cries from above, this time more insistent. *It is time to leave.* I have just found a hot spot that seems to be producing well, but I have no way of communicating this to Pete. I gather my bag of assorted goodies and begin groping above me for the exit to this blackened vault. Visibility is virtually zero and I am just able to make out Pete's dive light after standing upright, my head a scant foot from the room's ceiling. Unable to see the hole through which I entered, I reach upward and grab Pete's light, relying upon him to pull me up and out of the mess I have spent the last few minutes creating. Without Pete to guide me to the exit, I would have been hopelessly lost within this dark cauldron, unable to find my way out. As he pulls me up by my extended arm, I gesture to him and point at the contents of my mesh bag. Pete in turn gestures and points to his gauge console, showing me that we have been on the bottom for eighteen minutes, and that it is time to get out of here!

————

————

Pete has tied the ascent line to the deck railing, and we begin our slow return to the surface. This kind of teamwork is essential in diving the *Choapa,* and I am thankful that this ascent line is set up as I drag the heavy bag of artifacts up with me. Finally reaching our first de-compression stop at 30 feet, we begin what will be 40 minutes of

Tom Packer's search for the **Choapa's** *bell yielded only half of the prize—the bell was apparently broken in half, perhaps by a falling cargo boom, during the ship's sinking. Part of the letter "H" is visible to the left—the bell was marked with the ship's original name,* Helga. *Photo by author.*

hanging on this thin line tethering us to the wreck below. Only now are we able to more carefully examine the few treasures we have liberated from the Chilean freighter. Some of the wine bottles still have their contents intact, even after some 40 years of immersion in the hostile sea. We have recovered bottles of both red and white wine. There is a small pie plate with a blue flag emblazoned upon its rim, but I am heartbroken to discover that the wine glass I found at the very end of the dive has been broken by the heavy mass of bottles that I stuffed into the bag in my earlier frustration. Damn! I should know better than to place such a delicate object in with all those bottles. I vow to myself not to repeat this mistake.

We have since made numerous visits to the *Choapa* and she becomes more familiar with each return, though she never seems glad to see us. Much more china has been brought to the surface since our first successful exploration of her bridge section. In all we have discovered four distinctly different patterns of china. In addition to the first discovered and easily the most common "CSAV" blue-flagged china, there is china emblazoned in black with a crest inscribed "SOC-ANON-MTMA-GONZALEZ SOFFIA YC$^{\underline{A}}$." Another type, quite rare, is decorated in a purplish color, a small pennant with the letter "J" in its center and the vessel's home port of Valparaiso printed below it. The fourth type of china appears to be a holdover from the ship's previous owners, J. Lauritzen, for whom the ship was originally built. Its simple design sports only an elegantly scripted "JL."

Built in 1937 at Elsinore, Denmark, by Helsingors Jernsk & Msk. for J. Lauritzen, she was originally named the *Helga*. She was sold to the Chilean government in 1941, under whose ownership she was operated by Compania Sud-Americana de Vapores as the *Choapa*, at which time her home port was Valparaiso, Chile. She was quite a small ship, measuring only 292 feet long and 1700 gross tons. At the time of her sinking, she was on a voyage from Valparaiso to New York with a cargo of sugar. Judging by the huge quantity of wine and beer bottles found inside the ship's bridge, it can only be assumed that she possessed a very happy crew!

The
Continuing
Salvage
of the
Andrea Doria

———

———

———

———

———

———

———

———

———

———

———

———

The entire hull shuddered violently as it crashed back into the angry, confused sea. The boat had just leapt off the back of another huge breaker, momentarily airborne before smashing her keel back into the trough of the huge waves. I couldn't help but wonder just how much more pounding the boat or its passengers could take. The seas were running 12 to 15 feet and coming at us from the starboard stern quarter—the northeast gale was in full swing. At times the sea picked up the 35-foot Maine Coaster *Seeker* and tossed her across the ocean's raging surface with the ease of a child skipping a stone across a small pond. The gale had blown up from out of nowhere early this morning and now had us at its mercy far from any safe harbor; we would have to ride it out at sea.

Dennis Kessler and I had begun our third dive in two days on the wreck of the *Andrea Doria* at seven o'clock that morning. The ocean then gave no hint of what was to come only a few short hours later; her surface had been marred only by a slight chop as we entered the water. By the time we had completed our dive and climbed back on board, however, the slight chop had built up to a solid 5-foot sea, and the wind was steadily increasing. The dive flag flying overhead was snapping violently in the freshening breeze, sounding as if it would tear itself to threads at any moment. As we climbed back on board the *Seeker*, we were told that Captain Steve Bielenda of the R/V *Wahoo* had radioed us from Montauk Harbor on the Single Side Band. He told us that there was a full gale on the way, and that we had better get under way as soon as possible. But a quick retreat from the wreck of the *Andrea Doria* is impossible. She lies 100 miles east of Montauk Point, New York, and some 60 miles south of the remote and shoal-encircled island of Nantucket—a long way home for a small boat.

We were now being pounded relentlessly by the huge seas, which were constantly testing our small boat to its limit. The waves seemed mountainous. The horizon disappeared from sight each time the boat dropped into a trough and we were engulfed by a vast wall of blue and frothy white. Riding out a gale in a small boat far offshore is uncomfortable and physically abusive, but now simple survival had become a real concern. The trip between the wreck of the *Andrea Doria* and Lake Montauk is a 12-hour run in ideal weather; under these conditions there was no telling how long it would take to reach port, if indeed we made it at all.

For endless hours we clung to the seats in the small cabin, trying to tell jokes and make light of the situation. We silently prayed that time would speed up and pass more quickly—but there would be no quick end to this torturous roller coaster ride. Fatigued by the long hours of continuous pounding, we climbed into the *Seeker*'s cramped bunks and attempted to sleep. But the stifling heat below combined with the boat's violent motion made slumber impossible; the berths had become just another place on board to pass the time. Our breath hitched each time we were tossed into the air as the boat lurched off the top of another passing crest. Momentarily weightless, we soon crashed back into the bunks with gut-wrenching force. All we could do was lie there and wait for the next wave to come along and repeat the cycle.

The magnitude of the beating taken by both crew and boat on this journey home is perhaps best evidenced by the ice chest of Budweiser we had carefully nurtured for three days, doing our best to keep its contents cold in the summer heat. During our 16-hour ordeal in the teeth of the gale, we hadn't felt up to even approaching the ice chest. While no one was actually seasick, most of us had certainly felt better (later on we decided that we had been too scared to get sick). After finally reaching port and jumping off the boat, we spent a few minutes stumbling about like drunks, unaccustomed to walking on dry, stable land. Our ordeal over, we headed for the cooler full of icy, cold beer. Much to our humorous chagrin, however, we were confronted by a cooler full of stale, flat beer with 48 empty bottles rolling about its bottom. Every single bottle of beer had blown its top off during the course of the trip home in those tumultuous seas!

Several hours later, enjoying an early morning (2 A.M.) breakfast at a diner in Southampton, we were finally able to more peacefully reflect upon the events of the last several days. Four of us sat in the small booth, gently swaying to-and-fro to some unheard rhythm, still reacting to the motion of the restless sea. Now safe and warm but still dazed from the experience, we were quite happy to have made the trip. After all, we had finally succeeded in our quest to retrieve china from the *Andrea Doria*.

———

———

In fame, the sinking of the *Andrea Doria* is outshone only by the fate of the *Titanic* and the *Lusitania*. While the *Titanic* shocked the world by her incredible loss of life, and the *Lusitania* by the apparent barbarism of those responsible for her destruction, the *Andrea Doria* shocked the world by the mere fact that such a calamity could occur in modern times. While she was not publicly proclaimed unsinkable like the *Titanic* before her, she was unconsciously considered to be so, if not by her modern, compartmentalized design, then certainly by the advanced technological age into which she was born. The climate in which her sinking occurred was reminiscent of that leading to the *Titanic's* end; man in his arrogance had once again come to believe that his technology and machines were superior to the forces of nature. It seems that we must be periodically reminded that we cannot completely master the world around us, that we must ultimately bow down and yield to nature's divine force or be destroyed in the attempted resistance. This lesson seems to be repeated again and again throughout history.

The events of July 25 and 26, 1956, have been told countless times by many authors. Two excellent books that tell the story in its entirety are Alvin Moscow's *Collision Course* and William Hoffer's *Saved!* Both of these works tell the stories of the passengers and crew in minute detail and make excellent reading. A brief summary of the collision is all that will be attempted here, and the reader is referred to the excellent works of the above authors for a more complete account.

A calm, foggy night found two ocean liners, the Italian line's *Andrea Doria* and the Swedish line's *Stockholm* steaming toward one another at very nearly full speed. Though each ship detected the other on their respective radar sets, destiny was not to be changed

At 11:10 P.M. on July 25, 1956, the Swedish liner Stockholm *sliced deeply into the side of the Italian liner* Andrea Doria, *sending her to the bottom the following day. The accident provided the beginning for what would become an endless parade of explorers and would-be salvagers. Drawing by C. G. Evers, courtesy of George Hoffman.*

that night. At 11:10 P.M. on July 25, the bow of the *Stockholm* sliced a deep and fatal wound in the starboard side of the Italian liner. Eleven hours later, at 10:09 A.M., July 26, 1956, the most beautiful ocean liner then afloat finally succumbed to her fate and vanished from the surface of the sea forever. But the *Andrea Doria* did not vanish from memory; rather, her fateful demise would prove to be only the beginning of her story. Now lying on the ocean floor under 250 feet of icy, turbid water, she would prove to have more allure for many than she did during her short three-year career plying the North Atlantic passenger routes.

The great ship did not lie long on the bottom before her first visitors arrived to behold her in her new and final resting place. It took a mere 27.5 hours after she disappeared beneath the waves for

Peter Gimbel and Joseph Fox to arrive at the scene of her sinking, intent on photographing her as she lay on the bottom. They anchored their chartered, twin-screw fishing boat *Waleth* next to a marker buoy thoughtfully left by the Coast Guard the previous day, donned their dive gear and eagerly rolled over the side. These first postmortem visitors to the wreck attempted no salvage; they came purely for the adventure involved and the opportunity to photograph her for *Life* magazine. Their hastily arranged visit to this new wreck was pure adventure every step of the way. They ran their boat through dense fog banks all the way to the wreck site, anchored in the middle of the same fog-blanketed shipping lanes that had caused the *Doria's* very demise, and then pushed the infant sport of scuba diving to its limits. The ending of their little venture could very well have been written by a Hollywood scriptwriter. On the trip home, Gimbel swam through a half-mile of pounding surf to gain the beach and fetch help; their chartered boat had run out of fuel just short of Nantucket Island. The photographs taken by Gimbel and Fox appeared in the pages of both the August 6 and August 13 issues of *Life* magazine, giving all the world a brief but sad glimpse of the once-stately liner lying stricken on the ocean floor.

Peter Gimbel was to become the most frequent, the most organized, and perhaps the most successful visitor to this awesome shipwreck. In 1956, after his first brief visit to the wreck site, he declared, "The *Andrea Doria* is a stirring, unbelievable thing to see . . . she seems almost alive." Although today she appears to be deep in slumber, she is still just as stirring and incredible a sight as she was then. And she is still very much alive.

Only two weeks later, Gimbel again set out for the *Doria*, in pursuit of more photographs, this time in color. Organized by Ken MacLeish of *Life* magazine, the excursion comprised two teams of divers, two cameras, and underwater lights for penetrating the wreck. Accompanying MacLeish and Gimbel were divers Bob Dill, Earl Murray, and Ramsey Parks, with Doctor James Stark of the U.S. Navy along in case of mishap. The trip to the wreck site was made aboard a 50-foot diesel cruiser complete with a portable decompression chamber in case of any trouble with the bends. Perhaps running out of fuel on the last trip had prompted the use of a larger and better equipped boat for this excursion.

The weather, a constant obstacle to overcome, permitted only three dives each by the two teams in a span of eight days. The Coast Guard's buoy no longer marked the site, so with the help of an airplane, they located the wreck by following her oil slick to the point where it, along with a steady stream of air bubbles, originated. During their dives they explored the interior of the wreck, including such areas as the First Class Observation Lounge, the after lounges and swimming pools, and the glass-enclosed Promenade Deck. The photographs taken by the divers during their underwater tour of the vessel appeared in the September 17, 1956, edition of *Life* magazine. This was also the first successful salvage attempt on the liner, with divers bringing up several random items from the ship, including a passenger's suitcase and a telephone.

Three weeks later, yet another expedition was making its way out to what was fast becoming a popular spot in the North Atlantic. The first attempt at cinematography of the ship as she lay on the bottom of the ocean was to be made by two veteran divers, Louis Malle and Frederic Dumas. The venture had been organized by Malle, James Dugan, and John F. Light, Jr., just two days after the *Doria*'s sinking. The many arrangements that had to be made coupled with the inclement weather had delayed their departure until September 12. Hurried arrangements for a boat, cameras, divers, and a portable decompression chamber had to be made. During the interval between planning the expedition and its departure, the team rented their decompression chamber to the Gimbel-Parks-Murray-Dill enterprise, only to watch them return from the wreck and publish color still photographs of the great liner that they, themselves, hoped to film.

When things finally came together for them, their chartered boat *Samuel Jamieson* departed, and just as others before them had done, they used the wreck's drifting oil slick to locate her. On the way out to the wreck site, one crew member reportedly rescued a cocktail olive that was drifting helplessly in the slick. Overcoming a temperamental fathometer, they located the huge ship and dropped a grapnel into her. Their first dive was planned mainly to make exposure tests

Dawn on July 26 found the Andrea Doria *listing heavily to starboard. Photo courtesy of The Mariners' Museum, Newport News, Virginia.*

in the dim twilight below. Swimming over the Promenade and Boat decks, Malle shot 20 seconds of film while Dumas recovered a grey metal ashtray, complete with a cigarette butt still in place. Visibility was murky, the water was cold, and a strong current made lugging the heavy camera about the wreck an exhausting task.

"It is a brainless place down there," Dumas said. "You are absolutely stupid with rapture of the deep. You can only try to keep a small fire in your brain to get you out of there alive."

The exposure tests completed, the filming was to begin in earnest the following day. But the North Atlantic becomes a fickle lady in September, and only a fool ignores her tantrums. During the night, the seas built steadily to 8 feet and the *Samuel Jamieson* and her divers were forced to return to port. Back in Nantucket, it would be six days before the weather would abate. A slave to previous commitments, their chartered vessel had to return to New York before they could return to the *Doria*. The ambitious divers soon located another vessel, however, though it was not large enough for the decompression chamber and, reluctantly, this had to be left behind. Finally returning to the wreck site, they found that their buoys had been torn loose by the seas and had disappeared. It was late in the day and the echo sounder was not working well when they finally grappled the wreck, so no attempt was made to determine where on the wreck their anchor lay.

They hurriedly dressed and began their long descent down the anchor line. They found the visibility very poor as they dropped steadily into the surrounding darkness. Reaching 160 feet, they expected to see the side of the great hull, but there was nothing but an inky blackness. Continuing downward, their senses numbed by nitrogen narcosis, they finally reached the end of their anchor line at a depth of 215 feet, where they found the grapnel caught in one of the ship's huge propellers. Though Malle attempted to capture something on film, it was a hopeless gesture in the deep, murky darkness that prevailed. Time is short at such great depths, and they quickly made their return to the surface empty-handed. As they climbed onto the boat after completing their lengthy decompression, it was discovered that Malle's eardrum had been ruptured during the dive. Their venture was over, with only 20 seconds of film and a tiny, grey metal ashtray to show for their efforts. "The sea owns the *Andrea Doria* now," exclaimed Dumas.

The rapidly approaching winter would now permit the *Doria* to lie peaceful and undisturbed on the bottom of the Atlantic until spring. This had been a busy and eventful year for her.

The following summer, shortly after the first anniversary of her sinking, Peter Gimbel and Ramsey Parks made a short return visit to the wreck. They had come back to examine the vessel and photograph the changes that had occurred during one year on the bottom of the harsh ocean. While they discovered that the wreck was now covered with barnacles and other marine growth, they found her name to be still visible on the bow. They spent most of their first two dives exploring and photographing the bridge area. While they had planned to make five or six dives on the wreck, they called off the remainder of the expedition after being attacked by a 12-foot shark while decompressing at the end of their second dive. The shark apparently came straight for Gimbel, who stabbed it in the head with his dive knife in a last-ditch defense. The shark didn't return, but then neither did the divers that year.

—————

—————

As time wore on, the great Italian liner faded slowly from the public's consciousness, though she was by no means forgotten by shore-bound dreamers and would-be adventurers. Schemes for raising the ship or salvaging her vast treasures abounded over the next several years. A brief stroll through the pages of history as told by *The New York Times* reveals but a few of these schemes, which were brought forth for public scrutiny; doubtless many more were planned in hushed tones over a few beers in countless taverns across the land.

TRENTON BID MADE TO REFLOAT DORIA
Salvager Offers to Buy Ship and Raise Her
by Ballast Method With Ore Boats
July 28, 1957

NEW OFFERS MADE TO BUY THE DORIA
No Agreements Signed Yet, Report Says,
Despite U.S. Teams Announcement
February 7, 1958

Plan to Salvage Doria Lacks Italian Approval
April 9, 1958

Virginian Would Raise Andrea Doria
October 15, 1959

All of these salvage plans fell by the wayside, however, and the *Doria* remained hidden in silent seclusion for nearly seven years. It would take a group of men with more than just fanciful visions of grandeur to open the doors to her treasure vaults. It would take men with daring and adventure in their hearts, and with the drive and desire to make their dreams come true. Such a group of divers was destined to take a crack at the greatest of modern shipwrecks during the summer of 1964.

During the winter months of 1963, an adventurous group of divers began formulating plans to salvage the great liner. The operation had the financial backing of two Washington, D.C., real estate business-men. This financial backing provided the group with the means to prepare the most ambitious salvage attempt yet on the *Doria*. They purchased and outfitted a 125-foot surplus Coast Guard cutter to use as their base of operations. She was outfitted with a myriad of gear, including air compressors, cable winches, all the necessary diving gear, and even an on-board decompression chamber. Their newly equipped salvage vessel was promptly named the *Top Cat*, and she was brought to her new home in New Bedford, Massachusetts, which would serve as her base of operations.

The work on the wreck was planned in three stages. The first phase would be to find and positively identify the wreck of the *Andrea Doria*. This in itself was a significant challenge. No one had visited the wreck site in almost seven years, and there were no longer any buoys marking her grave. Her exact location was unknown. The second phase of the project was to locate and bring to the surface the solid-bronze, life-size statue of Admiral Andrea Doria, which stood in the ship's First Class Lounge on the Promenade Deck. What the divers claimed to be the final phase of the operation was dramatic indeed: the salvors planned to bring the *Andrea Doria* herself back to the surface!

In the beginning of July 1964, phase one of the project began after long months of planning and preparation. Historically July and August are the only months when good weather in the region of the *Doria*'s sinking is reasonably certain. After months of research and investigation, the commander of the *Top Cat*, Captain Dan Turner, had come up with three completely different positions for the wreck. Due to the uncertainty of the *Doria*'s exact location and the primitive navigation aids available, it took two full days of searching to locate what appeared to be the wreck of the famed Italian luxury liner lying on the bottom of the ocean floor. Using a set of coordinates given to them by a Swedish trawler captain, they had found a large object lying beneath 250 feet of water. The wind was blowing fiercely with 10-foot swells rocking the *Top Cat*. By the morning of July 3, it was apparent that there would be no break in the weather. The three divers on board decided that they would attempt the dive despite the rough weather.

The three men descended down a marking buoy, which they dropped on what they hoped was the *Andrea Doria*. Fighting currents and rough seas all the way, the group finally came upon a huge ship lying on the ocean bottom. Landing atop a vast expanse of hull, all they could see was the ship's waterline and portholes fading into the distant haze. One of the three divers, Salvatore Zammitti later said, "In my heart I knew that this must be the *Andrea Doria*, but how in the world could I prove it?" To ensure their safe return to the surface, the divers didn't wander far from their descent line. All they could find in the vicinity to bring to the surface was what appeared to be a large, bronze lifeboat rudder. The three enterprising divers attempted to carry the 200-pound rudder up the descent line until they were finally forced to drop the heavy object half-way to the surface. Such heavy exertion is extremely dangerous at these depths, and the three were lucky that no mishap occurred in this foolish, hastily attempted salvage. Returning to the surface, the divers were disappointed that they were unable to identify the wreck, and they hoped to explore a more promising section of the vessel the following day. The weather grew steadily worse, however, and like others before them, the crew of the *Top Cat* were forced to return to port, leaving behind a large marker buoy to ensure the successful location of the wreck when they returned.

Back in New Bedford, the *Top Cat* was resupplied and a few minor repairs made while the crew awaited a break in the weather. When the good weather finally arrived, it was July 24. The *Top Cat* departed for the *Doria* with three new divers and one returning from the previous trip three weeks earlier. They were determined to identify the vessel and bring proof of its identity back to the surface. After a

12-hour trip out to the wreck, they found the sea conditions once again too rough to dive. They weathered 6-foot swells for two days before conditions improved enough to permit diving. This time Captain Turner made several passes over the wreck, using the fathometer to pinpoint the bridge area. Dropping a marker buoy on the spot he had picked out, Captain Turner joked that he had dropped the buoy right into the wheelhouse door for the divers. Sure enough, the first two divers to descend the marker line found that it led right to the wheelhouse door!

Over the course of the next week, the two teams of divers alternately battled fluctuating weather and nitrogen narcosis to recover various pieces of equipment from the ship's bridge. Among the equipment brought to the surface was a pelorus, found mounted in a binnacle on the port bridge wing. Photographs of this same binnacle, which had been taken during Gimbel's explorations of the wreck, had appeared in both the September 17, 1956, and the October 28, 1957, issues of *Life* magazine. Also recovered was the *Doria*'s port running light, a 1000-watt floodlight, and a radar set custom-made for the ship, thereby providing positive proof of her identity. Their identification task successfully completed, the group returned to port to prepare for phase two of their ambitious project.

On August 15, 1964, the *Top Cat,* with four divers aboard, departed New Bedford once again, this time to attempt the most enterprising salvage project to date on the *Doria.* They would attempt to locate and raise the life-size statue of the sixteenth century Italian military hero, Admiral Andrea Doria, after whom the luxurious liner was named. If the statue, which was considered to be one of the finest pieces of art on board, could be reclaimed from the sea, it would far surpass any other object yet brought up from the wreck.

The four divers on board the *Top Cat* were blessed with fine weather and made two to three dives a day for eight consecutive days in their efforts to free the statue from its precarious position in the ship's lounge. Once the divers had located the statue in the First Class Lounge, they blasted a hole through the wall of the Promenade Deck directly over the statue to give them direct access to the statue and greatly facilitate its removal. Working in teams, the divers cut the statue off at its ankles to free it from its mounting pedestal. Using lift bags, they raised the statue straight up to the surface through the newly cut hole in the hull. This was an incredible feat for four divers to accomplish in only eight days, with the entire operation being conducted using only scuba. The divers were increasingly harassed by sharks during their salvage efforts, and they managed to complete the operation just as the large porbeagle sharks became overly aggressive.

Returning to port with their prize, the *Top Cat* crew had just concluded the most ambitious and successful expedition to date on the wreck of the *Andrea Doria*. Although Captain Turner boasted that they would return the following year to raise the ship herself, it is doubtful that even he believed this. The crew of the *Top Cat* would not return to visit her again. The statue of the famous Italian admiral reportedly resides at a motel in Florida, while his sandal-clad feet still stand on their pedestal in the *Doria*'s First Class Lounge—a lasting testament to the salvage effort by the crew of the *Top Cat*.

———

———

The headline in *The New York Times* on, Monday, May 27, 1968:

DIVERS TO SURVEY THE ANDREA DORIA
Inspection of Sunken Liner Planned by 5-Man Team

This headline boldly announced yet another visionary quest to the great wreck lying south of Nantucket Island. This time a team of four Italians and one American would conduct a survey of the ship, taking motion pictures while investigating the feasibility of salvaging her. The expedition was organized and led by Bruno Vailati, an Italian television producer and director. The survey team included Cosmo Dies and Arnaldo Mattei as topside tenders, with Vailati, Stefano Carletti, and the lone American, Al Giddings, as divers.

Bruno had chartered the 95-foot fishing trawler *Narragansett* to take them out to the wreck site for three weeks. Vailati hoped to get enough underwater footage to use in a film series he was producing called *The Seven Seas*. The three divers made a total of 21 dives to the wreck, literally filming her from stem to stern.

Bruno's film, *Fate of the* Andrea Doria, is a most entertaining adventure. Somewhat over-dramatic and reminiscent of a home movie, it nonetheless has some fascinating underwater footage of the wreck. At the time it was shot, the ship's bridge and wheelhouse were still intact, and the resulting rare footage of this part of the wreck is fascinating to a diver who has been there more recently. All that is now left of the bridge where Captain Calamai once commanded this great vessel is the skeletal remains of the port bridge wing. Below this lies a vast, empty void shrouded in abandoned fishing nets and cloaked in the eternal twilight of the ocean depths.

Vailati had a complicated but highly effective system for the divers' decompression. They used a small Boston Whaler and a weighted shot line to transfer the decompressing divers from the buoyed descent line to a set of decompression lines hanging beneath the *Narragansett*. Here each of the divers had his own oxygen line to aid his decompression. Lines were lowered from above to take the divers' heavy cameras, and they even had a shark cage available to protect them from the marauding intruders. While this system worked well, all the dives were being made on scuba with its short bottom times and lengthy in-water decompression. If any serious attempts at salvaging the vessel or its riches were to be made, some other method allowing more bottom time would have to be found.

While Bruno Vailati and his team were out filming the wreck, another team was proceeding with their own salvage preparations. Alan Krasberg and Nick Zinkowski had come up with the necessary equipment to greatly extend their working bottom time on the wreck. Employing the technique of saturation diving, first tested on humans in the open sea in 1962, the divers' bottom time could theoretically be extended indefinitely, decompressing only once at the end of the expedition. Krasberg designed and built an underwater habitat named *Early Bird,* which would be moored to the wreck for the duration of the project. Two divers could live in the habitat for up to a week at a time. Living at a depth of 160 feet, the divers would reach equilibrium with the surrounding pressure after about 24 hours, and daily decompression would be unnecessary as long as they returned to their habitat rather than to the surface after each dive. Thus the divers' bottom time now was limited only by their air supply, which would be provided through long hoses from the surface support vessel, where thousands of cubic feet of gas could easily be stored. Such an operation is expensive and dangerous. Should anything go wrong during a dive or if something happened to the habitat, retreat to the surface was impossible. Once saturated, the divers could only return to normal sea level pressure slowly, requiring two full days of decompression. An emergency ascent to the surface meant a swift and certain death from explosive decompression sickness; their blood would literally boil with dissolved gas coming rapidly out of solution. The divers' lives literally depended upon the integrity of their habitat.

This operation was being conducted on a shoestring budget. Perhaps no better indication of this exists than the construction of their habitat, *Early Bird.* Krasberg had designed and built the underwater dwelling out of eight-by-twelve-inch fir planking impregnated with a sealant of polyester resin. Building a dependable pressure vessel out of wood planking is a seemingly impossible task. Trusting one's life to its integrity is highly risky at best. A major leak or seal blowout would spell instant death to the divers inside. Building such a structure of wood and attempting a saturation operation of this magnitude using it as the major life support system must either be admired for its incredible daring and courage or looked upon as an act of sheer lunacy.

The group's plan was to moor *Early Bird* to the hull of the *Doria* at about 160 feet and use this as their base of operations as they cut through two steel doors in the side of the hull. Once they gained access to the ship's interior, they planned to locate the purser's safe, cut through its doors and reclaim the safe's contents. They also hoped to bring up as much china and silverware as they could find, with the intention of auctioning it in New York, where they expected it would fetch a high price among souvenir collectors. Accompanying the expedition was a film crew of Al Giddings, Jack McKenney, and Chuck Nicklin, as well as two photographers from *Life* magazine.

The major flaw in the execution of the team's scheme was their timing. It is well known that there are only two months out of the year (July and August) when reasonable weather can be expected in this region of the Atlantic. Yet the chartered catamaran *Atlantic Twin*, towing the *Early Bird* behind it, didn't leave port for the wreck until October 2. October is well into hurricane season, and it is an awful month to conduct an extended offshore operation such as this. The miserable weather combined with a few serious mechanical problems caused Krasberg to postpone the project indefinitely before the habitat *Early Bird* was put into operation. The only diving actually done were a few working dives by Krasberg and Zinkowski, as well as some photographic dives by the film crew. All of these dives were done on ordinary scuba. The saturation system designed to extend their bottom time on the wreck was never tested, and the entire operation was yet another failed attempt to salvage the great Italian liner.

While the *Early Bird* expedition had been a failure, it had opened the door to a new era of diving on the *Doria*. From now on, saturation diving would play an important role in efforts at salvaging the wreck. The next team of divers to employ the saturation technique was successful operationally, although they were not at all successful in their quest to salvage the ship's vast riches. In July of 1973, two young Navy divers, Chris DeLucchi and Don Rodocker, began their own attempt at salvaging the wreck that seems to have drawn more salvors than any other in recent memory. DeLucchi and Rodocker would also attempt to employ the technique of saturation diving to greatly extend their working time on the wreck. They formed a firm called Saturation Systems, Inc., and managed to interest enough investors to enable them to build a proper habitat of steel, constructed according to both American Society of Mechanical Engineers and Coast Guard codes. The resulting habitat, nicknamed

Mother, was capable of supporting three divers at a maximum depth of 600 feet for up to 21 days. The divers were to breathe a mixture of helium and oxygen (heli-ox) to combat the disorientating effects of nitrogen narcosis that normally occur at the depths at which they would be working. They would also wear hot-water suits to protect them from the numbing cold of the deep Atlantic.

The divers had chartered the fishing trawler *Narragansett,* no stranger to the *Andrea Doria,* as their support vessel. Along to document the expedition was a four-man photographic team consisting of Bob Hollis, Jack McKenney, John Clark, and Bernie Campoli.

After numerous mechanical problems, which at one point forced the *Narragansett* to return to port for repairs on the habitat, the team managed to secure the saturation complex to the side of the *Andrea Doria.* Five days after entering the habitat, DeLucchi and Rodocker finally managed to cut a 4-foot-square hole through the doors leading into the First Class Foyer. From here they hoped to gain access to the purser's safe, as well as the jewelry shop, bank, and chapel of the elegant liner. To their dismay, they found the dark interior of the wreck in a total shambles. Wall and ceiling panels had fallen from their supports and hung precariously from dangling electrical cables, waiting to fall on an unsuspecting diver. Fine silt covered every surface, and much of the interior appointments had fallen from their proper place in the ship and lay in a jumbled heap on the deep side of the wreck. The divers concluded that tons of rubble and debris would have to be removed to get to the purser's safe. Considering the dangers involved, along with the time and cost elements, they called off the entire venture. *Mother* was hauled back to the surface and towed back to Fairhaven, Massachusetts.

The only items actually recovered from the wreck were several silver-plated serving platters and an intact bottle of perfume found by Rodocker while exploring the Winter Garden area on the Promenade Deck. During an excursion to the bridge area on this exploration of the wreck, Bob Hollis discovered that the bridge itself had fallen away from the main hull, leaving only the port bridge wing behind. When Hollis dropped down to explore the wheelhouse, he was greeted by nothing but empty space. The years of corrosive action and the currents constantly tugging at the ship's superstructure must have finally ripped it free from the main hull, depositing it on the ocean floor somewhere below. The wheelhouse was destined to be rediscovered by none other than Peter Gimbel during his next exploration of the one shipwreck he couldn't stay away from.

Since Gimbel's first dive to the *Doria* in 1956, he had become a successful filmmaker, having produced and directed the film *Blue Water, White Death*. Now looking for new subject matter, Gimbel was inspired by his old obsession with his favorite shipwreck. Finding sponsors to finance his return to the wreck, he planned on filming a documentary about the ship and then airing it on national television. He chartered the vessel *G. W. Pierce* for the project. Gimbel and Al Giddings were to be the underwater cameramen, with Jack McKenney available as a backup if needed. As it turned out, McKenney would be called into action after Giddings ruptured an eardrum while decompressing in rough seas.

Gimbel hired the commercial firm of International Underwater Contractors (IUC) to supervise the diving operation. The commercial outfit brought to the operation a diving bell for completing the required lengthy decompressions, as well as the necessary surface-supplied diving gear to deliver a tri-mix breathing mixture of oxygen, nitrogen, and helium to the divers. The gas mixture would eliminate the effects of nitrogen narcosis, allowing the divers to think clearly at depth, and the surface umbilicals would provide the divers with a virtually unlimited supply of gas. This system would give each camera crew a bottom time of about an hour each day. The price for this amount of time on the wreck would be extremely long decompression times, split between the icy waters of the Atlantic and the relative comfort of the cramped diving bell. On occasion, these decompression times exceeded five hours!

On one dive, Gimbel and Ward Wright of IUC located the bridge wreckage of the vessel lying in the sand a short distance out from the hull. Now mostly broken rubble, it was covered with fishing nets. They did manage to find some recognizable features and filmed the bridge equipment and a lifeboat amid the rubble.

Jack McKenney spent several dives exploring the First Class Foyer, gaining access through the hole cut by Saturation Systems in 1973. Here he filmed the large central staircase, the glass doors leading into the ship's gift shop, and the enormous pile of debris that had fallen to the ship's starboard side. Bathroom fixtures were and still are one of the few recognizable features left in the ship's interior, and while filming them, they found the faucets to be in working order. McKenney also spent time filming some of the outside features of the wreck such as the propellers and the name "Andrea Doria" spelled out on the ship's bow.

Gimbel, on the other hand, was most interested in discovering why the ship had flooded so quickly after the collision. In fact, this was to become his obsession, inspiring the name of the expedition's resulting documentary, "The Mystery of the *Andrea Doria*." One of the theories advanced over the years to explain the rapid flooding of the generator room aft of the collision point was that a watertight door at the end of a tunnel connecting the flooded deep-tank compartment and the generator room was missing or bolted open. This negligent condition was rumored to have doomed the vessel from the moment of impact to her final place in history. Gimbel's own personal objective was to penetrate the wreck, locate the doorway, and either dispel or substantiate the rumor.

Exploring the impact area where the *Stockholm* hit is difficult since the *Doria* lies on her starboard side, the actual breach in the hull buried in the sandy ocean floor. Earlier attempts at penetrating aft from the forward cargo hold by Al Giddings had proven unsuccessful. Gimbel now decided to attempt to gain access to the area through a large crack discovered in the bottom of the hull at the collision point. This crack was found to be much larger than expected, extending almost one-third of the way across the ship's bottom. Attempts to penetrate this hull crack, however, were also unsuccessful, due to the extensive jumble of wreckage. While Gimbel did find hull damage that was much more extensive than previously believed, he failed to accomplish one of the primary goals of the expedition, and the mystery of the doorway would haunt him for six years, until he finally returned to solve the puzzle.

On July 29, 1981, the *Sea Level 11* left Montauk, New York, and headed out to the wreck site of the *Andrea Doria*. Aboard was a saturation-diving complex owned and operated by Oceaneering International under charter to Peter Gimbel. This would be his final assault on the great liner.

Gimbel's real reason for returning was his own nagging desire to solve the mystery of the generator room door: did it exist or not? Realizing, however, that the public and television networks wouldn't buy another documentary on that subject, he proceeded under the guise of a treasure hunt, an expedition to find and recover two of the ship's safes. By opening the safes on live television, and by airing the film, he hoped to capture the public's attention and spark enough interest to sell the event to the networks, all the while fulfilling his personal quest to solve the mystery that still plagued him.

Gimbel spent just over one month working the wreck, calling it quits for good on September 2. In that time he accomplished two of his major goals: he recovered the Bank of Rome Safe from the First Class Foyer Lounge, and he finally solved, to his own satisfaction, the mystery of the water-tight door, and the reason that the *Doria* filled so rapidly. His third objective of recovering the Purser's safe was just not possible in the allotted time.

After arriving at the wreck site, now a familiar spot in the North Atlantic, setting up the saturation system, and securing down lines to the wreck, the divers' job was to cut away the doors leading into the First Class Foyer Lounge. This was actually just an enlargement of the smaller hole cut by Saturation Systems back in 1973. (Gimbel seems to have taken considerable trouble in editing his resulting film to omit and even hide this fact, leaving the uninformed viewer to conclude that his diving team was the first to enter this area.) This enlargement left a huge hole in the side of the hull literally the size of a two-car garage door, giving future generations of amateur divers easy access to the interior.

After removing the exterior doors, the saturation team began the formidable task of digging through a mountain of rubble lying against the starboard side of the ship. After days of digging and removing debris, using various jury-rigged tools and brute force,

Drew Ruddy managed to locate the Bank of Rome safe at the bottom of the deep trench dug by the divers. Once located, it took several days to cut it free, rig it, and bring it to the surface to once again see the light of day.

Now that Gimbel's publicity stunt was completed with the recovery of the safe, he was able to turn his attention to his own personal obsession. He and Ted Hess had devised a scheme to get to the generator room from the Foyer Deck. Ripping off the front of the souvenir shop in the First Class Foyer, Hess cut a hole through the back of the souvenir shop to a large ventilator shaft running vertically through the ship. Swimming down through this shaft, the two divers finally managed to reach the generator room. Here they discovered that the water-tight door question was irrelevant—they found a huge hole in the outside of the ship's hull leading directly into the generator room. The *Stockholm* herself had pierced the compartment, causing it to flood instantaneously. The ship was doomed from the moment of the collision.

Running out of time, the expedition was brought to a halt in the beginning of September before the purser's safe could be located. The resulting film, Andrea Doria: *The Final Chapter* , was aired on television, its ratings undoubtedly boosted by the accompanying live opening of the recovered safe. The safe was found to contain paper currency, both American and Italian. After preservation, this currency was offered for sale to the public as souvenirs from the most intensely salvaged shipwreck of modern times.

Peter Gimbel died on July 12, 1987, after a long illness. He was, without doubt, the most persistent visitor, and probably the most successful salvager of the shipwreck that became his own personal obsession. From his photographs in *Life* magazine taken the day after her tragic sinking, to his final film 25 years later, he attempted to share with us his own fascination with the incredible world of the *Andrea Doria*. For this he will always be remembered fondly.

Diving the Wreck Today

_____

Despite the title of Peter Gimbel's last film, the final chapter on the *Andrea Doria* has not yet been written. Early each July a few privately chartered dive boats make the long journey east from Montauk, New York, to the *Doria*'s resting place. A handful of amateur sport divers are seeking adventure exploring the most famous shipwreck reachable with ordinary scuba gear. All who make the trek share a common bond—a love of the sea, of diving, and of exploring sunken ships. They are a daring lot with years of diving under their belts, willing to accept the risks involved to touch a piece of history. Driven by

some deep-seated lust from within—a need to explore the unknown—they come to experience what is perhaps the ultimate
wreck dive.

The trip itself is no ordinary dive charter, but rather takes on the
epic proportions of an expedition. The wreck lies far out to sea, some
100 miles and a 12-hour boat ride east of Montauk, New York. Best
attempted in early July when the seas are relatively mild, the 3-day
excursion begins with the loading and provisioning of a small
charter boat with enough food and water to sustain the approximately 20 people on board for the duration. Fuel tanks are topped off
to ensure an adequate supply for the long journey. Stacks of dive
gear, photographic and video equipment, as well as clothing and
other personal items are crammed into every corner of the boat. More
than 160 scuba cylinders are loaded on board for the planned four
dives on the wreck, should the unpredictable weather permit the full
agenda to be completed. All too often, however, heavy seas and near
gale-force winds force the intrepid divers to abandon the wreck site
and scurry for the safety of the nearest sheltered harbor. Yet, on other
occasions, the sea remains calm and lake-like for the entire three
days, providing a peaceful base for the intensive diving operations
for which all have traveled so far.

The magic of adventure is present throughout every phase of the
trip. Perhaps it is enhanced by being so far at sea with no immediate
shelter or readily available human assistance. The camaraderie
among the participants is surely another important aspect of the
venture. Divers travel from all corners of the country to visit the
elegant liner. Old friends met on last year's trip are greeted warmly
as we are reunited once again in our common quest. Old stories are
laughingly told and retold as we look forward to the promise of
another successful trip and the making of new stories.

Further allure is added by the incredible variety of marine life
present in the offshore waters in which the great liner lies. Sights
most often seen only at Marineland or on the pages of *National
Geographic* abound. Often on the journey to and from the wreck site,
schools of Atlantic dolphins appear out of nowhere, frolicking and
playing in the boat's bow wave. All on board take pleasure in these

playful yet wild animals, snapping pictures as fast as they can, for all too soon the dolphins vanish as quickly and mysteriously as they arrived.

On one expedition the boat was literally surrounded at intervals for two days straight by pods of pilot whales. Hundreds of the magnificent animals could be seen lazily making their way toward some unknown destination, paying little heed to the stranger anchored among them. On another trip, an endless parade of basking sharks made their way slowly past our small boat. Traveling both singly and in pairs, the huge plankton eaters undoubtedly traversed the flat seas for countless days beyond the two we spent in their domain. Living out an episode from a Cousteau film, we were permitted to approach to within arm's length of the giant creatures in our Zodiac before spooking them. With a seemingly effortless swoosh of their great tails, they disappeared into the depths, leaving behind only a gentle swirl to mar the glassy surface of the sea. Other often-seen deep-sea beasts include the huge but graceful finback and minke whales, the strange ocean sunfish or mola-mola, and, of course, the ever-present blue sharks, intent upon patrolling their home waters. And, yet, all of these experiences are mere fringe benefits to our real purpose in traveling so far from the safety of our land-locked lives.

Anticipation gives way to both excitement and anxiety as we near our destination, an anxiety borne of the danger inherent in the undertaking. There is an aura of mystery and peril surrounding the *Andrea Doria,* for here lies a magnificent, and, despite her many past visitors, largely unexplored giant among shipwrecks. She lies in a realm in which we are mere visitors, largely unwelcome and surely at odds with the hostile environment. Several have lost their lives exploring her, and no one wishes to follow suit. Yet the allure she holds for wreck divers is inescapable. Countless divers have sworn they were through with her, only to find themselves signing on for next year's trip after a long, dry winter, driven by some inner need to explore her captivating remains "just one more time."

The most impressive thing about diving the *Doria,* and indeed the one that first strikes a new visitor, is her immense size. Lying on the great wound in her starboard side, she at times seems like a huge skyscraper lying prone and strangely out of place on the ocean floor. I must constantly remind myself that this colossal giant is actually a ship, built by human hands. Landing on a flat expanse of hull after the seemingly endless descent to her side from the distant surface, I often marvel at the flatness of her hull for as far as I can see. She is so large that, even in the best of visibility, the curvature of her hull seems to elude the eye, and she seems an endless expanse of smooth, steel plating. Only upon approaching the uninterrupted run of the Promenade Deck along the side of the great ship is this monotony broken. The Promenade Deck appears as a deep gully cut in the immense stretch of steel hull plates. Once a glass-enclosed walkway stretching the length of the liner's superstructure, its windows have long since fallen or have been removed by divers. Crossing the Promenade Deck and daring to peer over her side, a diver is greeted by the lower Boat Deck and an inky blackness beyond it, for the ocean floor still lies some 80 feet below.

On only one occasion have I been permitted to grasp an overview of the wreck in all its majesty. On an overcast, late June afternoon, the current fell slack, and the normal 20- to 30-foot visibility opened up to nearly 100 feet. As if an opaque curtain had suddenly been lifted, our descent to the stern of the great ship was greeted by a magnificent spectacle.

To our right we see the three towering decks of the liner's super-structure, while off to our left the rounded fantail curves gently toward the sand far below. Jutting menacingly from the gracefully curved hull is the port propeller shaft and, at its end, the immense, twisted blades of the propeller itself. Unable to resist its hypnotic spell, Richie Kohler and I cross the momentarily still void until we can reach out and touch the conical end of the great shaft. We find ourselves dwarfed by this twisted monstrosity, and as I drop down-ward to a perch on the ship's rudder, I struggle to capture both the propeller in its entirety and my dive partner in the camera's viewfinder. Separated by a void of dark but clear water, we both marvel at how small we appear in contrast to this huge behemoth.

Seen up close, each blade of the Doria's *propeller is covered with sea anemones. Few divers have seen the propeller of this famous shipwreck. Photo by author.*

After snapping a few photos, we swim off to explore another corner of the vast ship like children let loose in an immense playground.

Ascending the ship's hull and crossing over her upper decks, we swim forward to the after cargo boom and drop over the sheer vertical face now formed by the Tourist Class Lido Deck. While Richie poses next to the huge boom, I drop downward along the deck, attempting to frame the two in my viewfinder. The cargo boom is now enshrouded by a serpent-like wrapping of massive fishing nets, draping downward toward the ocean floor. I drop further, until I find myself opposite the Tourist Class swimming pool, which appears oddly empty and yet full at the same time. Glancing downward, I can make out the vague outline of the starboard railing against a backdrop of sandy ocean floor. I feel an overwhelming compulsion to continue my descent to the bottom; what an incredible sight it must be to view the ship's stern looming overhead from such a vantage point. But the 250-foot depth is not in today's dive plan, and I force myself to concentrate on the task at hand. Returning my attention to the cargo boom overhead where Richie is waiting patiently, I continue my photographic efforts before returning to shallower waters.

Farther forward and just above the Promenade Deck lies the Boat Deck superstructure. Like lone trees hanging over the bluff of a high cliff, the port lifeboat davits stand, still in their retracted position. The immediate and severe list taken on by the *Doria* after her collision with the *Stockholm* prevented the use of the port lifeboats. It was impossible to lower them with the ship heeled over to such a great extent. Most of the lifeboats were ripped free when the great liner went down, and any that remained had long ago been torn loose from their davits by the strong ocean currents whipping over the ship's hull. But the davits remain as a mute testimony to the fact that only half the boats were usable at the time of the sinking. These same davits now support a canopy of abandoned fishing nets that billow over the Boat Deck below. The nets are one of the many hazards of diving the wreck, and must be given wide berth. Many are wrapped and twisted tightly about the wreck and pose no real hazard, but others sway gently in the current, waiting for an unwary diver to get careless and rise into their deadly embrace. On one visit to the wreck, I was hovering just forward of the severely decayed bridge wing, facing aft and concentrating on photographing my dive buddy Dennis Kessler silhouetted against the faint light from above. Suddenly he began to frantically flash his dive light at me, motioning for me to look behind. Turning about quickly, I half expected to be confronted by a roving shark intent on making me his next meal. Instead, I found an equally disturbing sight: the slight current that was carrying me slowly toward the bow was steering me straight into the clutches of a fine, nylon gill net, stretched out like a billowing sail in the current!

The strong ocean currents of the *Doria*'s resting grounds are one of the most perplexing problems involved in diving the wreck. Both the familiar Gulf Stream and Labrador currents exert their influence on the area, along with the clockwork flow of the ocean tides. It is almost an unheard-of occurrence to dive the *Doria* without the current significantly influencing the dive plan. This is, in fact, what made this dive's visit to the ship's propeller so incredible. In more than 30 dives on the wreck, I had never ventured out of arm's reach of the ship's hull, for fear of being swept up and carried away by the ever-present current. Yet, on this particular dive, the waters were still, allowing us to swim about unimpeded.

This water flow would almost be fascinating if we were able to view it from afar, rather than from within its clutches. Many a diver has surfaced from a visit to the *Doria* with arms weary from fighting the strong currents, clinging desperately to the boat's anchor line while decompressing. It often exists in levels, with a whipping current at the surface and none on the wreck below, or vice versa. At other times it is still or only slowly moving at both the surface and the bottom, but an intermediate stratum runs strongly under some unknown influence, dragging the anchor line along in a giant loop. But frequently it exerts its strongest influence on the bottom, where fighting it can be most hazardous. Often the only shelter from the water's movement is inside the wreck.

Venturing inside sunken ships is always a disorientating and hazardous adventure, but the *Andrea Doria* presents special challenges. The depth of the wreck alone is intimidating, for while the outside of the hull and the Promenade Deck can be reached at a relatively shallow 170 to 185 feet, any useful penetration of the ship's interior will take the diver to at least 200 feet, and perhaps much deeper. The position of the wreck on her side and the ever-present effects of nitrogen narcosis are disorienting. What was once the deck now becomes a wall, while what remains of the ship's walls and partitions are now the diver's floor. Cocktail tables jut out horizontally from the ship's deck like overgrown mushrooms. Thick electrical cables hang suspended like vines in some dark jungle. These cables present one of the most hazardous obstacles to anyone venturing inside the ship, and have claimed the life of at least one diver.

Another peril of entering the vessel is that of disturbing the layer of fine silt that covers every surface. It is impossible for even the most careful of divers to venture inside without agitating this carpet of

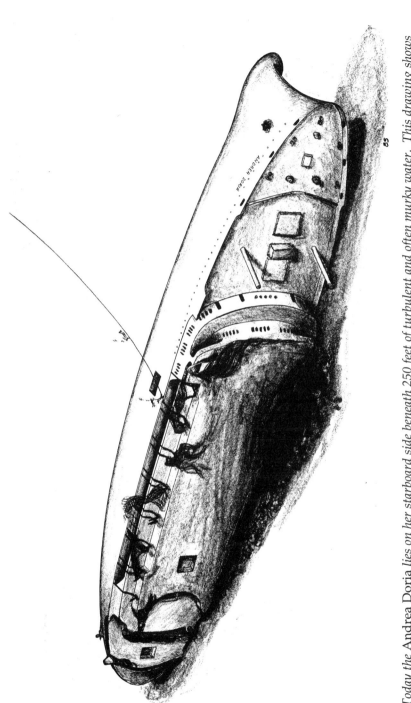

Today the Andrea Doria lies on her starboard side beneath 250 feet of turbulent and often murky water. This drawing shows the wreck as no diver has ever seen her—the ship's massive size makes it impossible to see her in her entirety even in the clearest water. Drawing by author.

sediment. Once disturbed, it instantly rises to form a blinding cloud in the dark interior, impenetrable by the most powerful of dive lights. The diver, now left in total darkness, must find his way out of this vast cavern by feel alone, relying on his memory of the landmarks he took note of on the way in, lest the *Doria* become his final tomb. The air supply carried on the diver's back is used up very quickly at the extreme depths of the *Doria*. If a diver should become lost in the interior, there is little time to search for the way out before his precious air dwindles away.

With all these dangers lurking inside the wreck, what lures the diver inside this dark cavern that was once the most beautiful ocean liner afloat? It is nothing other than adventurous speculation: the hope of recovering some small trinket among the vast treasures that went down with her on that fateful day in July. These treasures have no real monetary worth, but possess an intrinsic value to the salvor that transcends fiscal bounds. They represent a small piece of history, to be brought home as a reminder of an unforgettable visit to a magnificent lady.

When Peter Gimbel cut away the entrance doors into the First Class Foyer Lounge on his last visit to the wreck, he opened the way for sport divers to obtain their sought-after piece of history. Leading astern from the Foyer Lounge is a corridor that once led well-to-do passengers into the First Class Dining Room. The corridor is now dark and debris-laden, a confused jumble of decayed furnishings, cables, and linoleum flooring that has peeled away from the deck. But amid the diverse pile of debris have been found literally hundreds upon hundreds of dishes, bowls, cups, and crystal glasses: the first-class china that once served the wealthiest aboard. Gimbel's divers first discovered these treasures, leaving behind all but a very few pieces taken as personal souvenirs. What they left proved a bonanza for the divers who followed. What better artifact to bring back from a famous passenger liner than pieces of her first-class service? Penetrating the Foyer Lounge in search of dishes is a serious proposition, however, and is to be attempted only by the most advanced divers.

Following the trail blazed by many divers before us, Dennis Kessler and I make our own foray into the ship's interior in search of her china. Dropping through "Gimbel's hole," we descend vertically into the dark chasm below, the only illumination provided by the narrow beams of our dive lights. Passing the end of the steel partition that once enclosed the entranceway to the foyer, we begin swimming aft, angling downward toward the corridor where the sought-after prizes lie. Landing on the steel wall of the passageway at a depth of 205 feet, we check our air supply and bottom time, exchanging nervous glances before committing ourselves to entering the silty passageway. Swimming aft, we hug the deck side of the hallway, giving a wide berth to the numerous electrical cables draped along the remains of the ceiling. We come to a large, square opening in the "wall" that drops off below us into frightening blackness: it is the doorway that leads to the large central staircase.

Crossing this deep pit, we come finally to the "china mound," a jumbled pile of broken furnishings, bits of ceramic tile from the bathrooms overhead, and tangled webs of electrical cable, all inter-mixed with a 25-year accumulation of silt. We swim slowly aft, suspended a scant few feet above the debris field, our eyes carefully scanning the mound below for any sign of china. The easy hunting of several years ago when dozens of dishes lay clearly exposed for the taking has passed; we will have to dig for our bounty. It is obvious that we are hunting in the correct place, as a multitude of tubular plate racks lie strewn about below us.

We reach the entrance to the First Class Dining Room without spotting any exposed china—we have come far enough. Turning around and facing the direction we must follow to exit, we plunge our hands deep into the silt beneath us and blindly grope for the familiar form of a plate, cup or saucer. We are instantly engulfed in a blinding cloak of silt. The visibility quickly drops to zero, and even our powerful dive lights are unable to penetrate the enveloping murk. We are forced to keep one hand constantly on the floor alongside us to avoid becoming disorientated. Slowly we work our way back toward the entrance point, digging and probing blindly along the way in search of any small morsel the wreck might yield to us today.

Finally, reaching the deep chasm that is the entrance to the central staircase, we quickly cross it and leave our silt shroud behind us. Able to see with the aid of our lights once again, we check our bottom timers and see that we haven't much time left. We quickly examine our respective finds; Dennis has done better than I, but we have both gotten several intact pieces of china. This is not the place to admire our good fortune, however, and after securing our mesh bags, we head for the exit.

Swimming forward through the corridor, I find looking constantly upward for the exit hole to be the most nerve-racking part of the dive. Time is short, with only a few minutes remaining to regain the anchor line and begin our ascent. There is no time here for getting lost; a mistake might prove deadly. The huge hole in the hull left by Peter Gimbel appears as a tiny postage stamp far above, admitting a faint green light from the distant surface. It is a welcome sight when it comes into view, for it is our only means of escape from the ship's interior. Yet it would be premature to relax at this point. Until our decompression is completed and we are back safely on the boat, the dive remains an arduous test, a battle against the elements. Any momentary victory is tempered by the knowledge that the outcome could easily be different on the next dive.

For me, the next dive was a personal and demanding challenge, which had been building in me and begging for fulfillment for two long winters. Two years earlier, during an almost week-long sojourn on the wreck site spent aboard Captain Bill Nagel's boat *Seeker,* I had dropped deep into the *Doria's* interior in search of the Cabin Class Bar to find the crystal glassware that must have once filled this bar.

Dropping vertically downward into the Cabin Class Lounge from one of the open doorways in the Promenade Deck was a frightening experience. I found the lounge to be vast and inky black, devoid of any references or landmarks, save the seemingly infinite span of smooth, featureless flooring. The faint green glimmer of light from the doorway overhead was rapidly receding as I drifted slowly downward, ever deeper into the eerie, soundless abyss. Electrical

cables hung limply at intervals, looking like sinister serpents awaiting what would be my final mistake. Rapture of the deep began to
crowd my rational thoughts as I passed the 200-foot mark. Dennis
was stationed above at the entranceway, shining his dive light
downward to serve as a beacon to guide my way out again. It lent
little comfort to me, however, since it appeared as a tiny pinpoint of
light far overhead.

Reaching the centerline of the ship, I found the remains of the bar.
Against an otherwise featureless wall hung a 4-foot-long sink, its
triple faucet and drain pipe still in place. Abandoned by the fancy
appointments that once complemented its simple utility, it presented
a puzzling scene to my nitrogen-clogged mind. Where was the pile
of crystal glassware I had expected to find? Where was the rest of the
bar? Finally realizing that it must have slid downward to the deep
side of the wreck, I continued down in the desperate hope that it
might lay in a jumbled heap only a few feet below me. Reaching the
end of the wall on which the sink was mounted, I hung suspended
in space, shining my light into the endless abyss below me, too
frightened to go any farther. I gazed dully at the serpent-like cables
surrounding me. Straining to comprehend the reading on my depth
gauge, I did not care that it read 225 feet. Finally reaching the
conclusion that this was not the best of all possible places to be, I
turned and began ascending toward the pinpoint of light above.
Passing the sink, I wished that I had my camera with me, for I was
quite certain that no human eyes had beheld this scene in more than
25 years. Reaching Dennis at the entranceway, I followed him and
stationed myself at the next doorway aft as he dropped down to take
his turn at exploring the vast, as yet untouched interior of the *Andrea
Doria.*

This scene deep in the bowels of the wreck had haunted me for
two years, and now the time had come to return and photograph it.
Since we were anchored in Gimbel's hole, it would require a 150-foot
swim aft at a depth of 170 feet just to reach the doorway that leads into
the Cabin Class Bar. I would be making this dive alone, and would
not have the benefit of a diver stationed at the entranceway with his

light to help guide my way out again. After photographing the Cabin Class Bar, I planned on quickly photographing the remains of the First Class Bar as well, since it would be on my way back to the anchor line. If time permitted, I would complete my "bar-hopping" spree with a stop in the nearby cocktail lounge to photograph some of the glass-topped tables that still hung suspended from the floor. This was a very ambitious dive plan, and I would have to make every second count to fit it all into a single twenty minute dive.

———

———

In retrospect, I was very lucky that day: my "bar-hopping" adventure came off without a hitch. Everything went exactly as planned, and I accomplished everything I set out to do. I got my photographs of both bars and the cocktail lounge inside the *Andrea Doria*.

It was not a fun dive, but rather a frightening one. But at the time, under the given circumstances, it was the only way I could accomplish what I felt I must do.

For all of us who have visited her, the *Andrea Doria* lives on, and beckons us to return once again.

At 9:45 A.M. the great liner suddenly lurched over onto her side and begin to slowly settle by the bow—by 10:00 A.M. only her stern remained visible. At 10:09 A.M. she finally disappeared from view and settled to the ocean floor some 240 feet below. Photo by Harry Trask, courtesy of The Mariners' Museum, Newport News, Virginia.

The Doria's mammoth port propeller dwarfs diver Richie Kohler as seen from the rudder on a rare day of no current and spectacular visibility. Photo by author.

Draped in abandoned fishing nets, the Doria's *Boat Deck railing forms a ghostly silhouette when viewed from below. Photo by author.*

The port side lifeboat davits, still in their retracted position, remain as a ghostly reminder that only half of her lifeboats were useable at the time of the sinking. Photo by author.

Cathy Cush explores the Upper Deck near the vessel's stern. Photo by author.

Inside the ship, stairways present a disorienting maze to the diver, and are best left unexplored. The carpeting of sea anemones on the upper railing indicate that here, even deep within the wreck, the water is not stagnant—anemones can only flourish where there is a constant source of water-borne nutrients. Photo by author.

The elegant First Class Bar and Cocktail Lounge as they once appeared. Note the bar stools and glass-topped cocktail tables, which can still be seen today. Photo courtesy of Frank O. Braynard.

One of the glass-topped tables as it now appears inside the First Class Cocktail Lounge. Photo by author.

All that remains of the First Class Bar are these stools, which jut horizontally from the now vertical floor of the Cocktail Lounge. Photo by author.

A ling cod swims lazily along the ship's Tourist Class Promenade Deck. The teak decking throughout the vessel is still in remarkable condition, despite its long submergence. Photo by author.

The Cabin Class Bar and Cocktail Lounge can be found astern of its First Class counterpart, although it is not nearly as elegant. Photo courtesy of Frank O. Braynard.

This long sink, which hung behind the Cabin Class Bar, is still in place on its bulkhead. The bar itself has slid down to the deep side of the wreck. Photo by author.

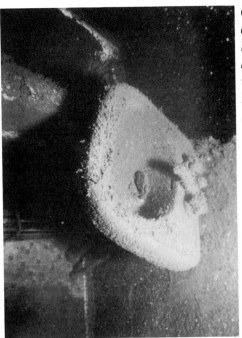

Outside the ship's Chapel on the Foyer Deck, bathroom fixtures hang absurdly alone—the walls which once enclosed them have long ago fallen away. Photo by author.

The vast void which forms the Tourist Class Dining Room is punctuated at neat intervals by dining tables fastened securely to the ship's now vertical deck. Photo by author.

Ed Sollner and Bruce Laden cling to the dive boat's anchor line while clutching a mesh bag of cups and saucers removed from a china cabinet in the ship's stern. Photo by author.

Mark Hill and Tom Christman display an assortment of Third Class cups and saucers recovered from the stern of the great liner. Photo by author.

The
Mystery
of the
Balæna

———
———
———
———
———
———
———
———
———
———
———
———
———
———

The enigma of the *Balæna* stands in strange contrast to the puzzling identity of the hundreds of unnamed wrecks littering the ocean floor. Poised on the brink of the treacherous "mudhole" east of Asbury Park, New Jersey, this shipwreck lies shrouded in intrigue. But unlike the mystery surrounding other wrecks, her true identity is known, for *Balæna* is not the fanciful christening of an imaginative fisherman, but her actual given name.

Years ago the ship's name was discovered when her large, bronze bell was brought to the surface, bearing the laboriously engraved inscription "BALÆNA." But here, where most stories begin, this one ends. Once the name of a shipwreck has been discovered, it is usually a fairly easy matter to find some record of her past. Archives, maritime registers, and similar historical sources contain a record of nearly all marine cataclysms. Yet the *Balæna* is unique. While many ships have been known to disappear without a trace, vanishing into the fog of history, the *Balæna* is a vessel that seems to have appeared out of this same fog; she stands before us as a ghost from the past with few clues to her origin or her demise. No one, to date, has been able to uncover her full story; no record of a ship known by this name sinking in the region has ever been found. She is like a time traveler from a distant age who remembers her own name and little else. We have few clues to work with in the search for details of her past. Her name, of course, is our major clue: the word "Balaena" (pronounced bayleena) originates in Latin and means whale. This leads us to the immediate speculation that she was a whaling vessel. Little additional evidence, however, has been gleaned from her remains since the discovery of her bell, and only clever detective work can lead us to any conclusions about her origins.

Her appearance on the bottom is quite impressive; she is in a remarkable state of preservation for a wooden-hulled sailing vessel. She sits perfectly upright on a dark, sandy bottom near the eastern slope of the mudhole, shrouded in dark twilight under 155 feet of clear yet tenebrous water. Other than her stern, which fades into silty, broken rubble mixed with a scattering of coal, apparently her final cargo, her hull seems entirely intact, with her rounded bow towering boldly some 20 feet above the bottom.

Many years ago, George Hoffman recovered this large bronze bell from a mysterious wooden sailing ship lying in 155 feet of water off the New Jersey coast. Inscribed with the name Balæna, *it triggered an inconclusive search through historical records for the fate of its owner. Photo courtesy of George Hoffman.*

Two huge masts lie felled beside her. The broken base of the forward mast rests on the starboard gunwale, with the remainder of the long spar sloping downward until it meets the surrounding

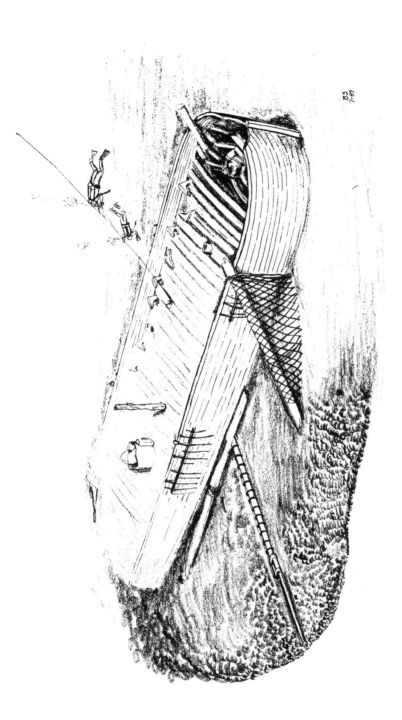

The wreck of the Balaena sits upright under 155 feet of dark water on the edge of the "mudhole." Beside her intact hull lie two of her masts, while her broken stern disappears into the silty ocean bottom. Drawing by author.

The vessel's forward mast is broken and lying on her starboard gunwale, and is draped with an abandoned fishing net. Photo by author.

bottom. Draped along its entire length is a large, abandoned fishing net. Farther back, near midships, lies a second mast, also to starboard and lying prone in the sand, stretching outward from the ship's hull. The mast's base still stands proudly upright on her deck. While the wooden spar is somewhat deteriorated, the lower mast is still bounded by iron hoops along its length. These hoops provide us with a clue to the vessel's rig. Such hoops on the lower mast were seldom used on fore-and-aft rigged vessels such as schooners, since they would interfere with the operation of the booms and gaffs supporting the

The remainder of the ship's main mast lies prone on the ocean bottom alongside her intact hull. The iron hoops surrounding the badly deteriorated wooden spar were used to bind together several pieces of timber to form a composite mast, saving on scarce and valuable lumber. Photo by author.

sails. This leads us to conclude that she was likely square-rigged. Both masts are of tremendous diameter, another indication of her stout build. Many deadeyes, both large and small, have been recovered from the wreck, remnants of the standing rigging used to support the great masts that once towered above her decks. The deadeyes recovered still have part of their stays attached. The stays are wire, not rope, indicating that she must have been built, or at least rerigged, sometime in the late 1800s. Wire was not used aboard ships for standing rigging until after the mid-nineteenth century. Yet a newly built ship rigged much later than this would have employed turnbuckles rather than deadeyes to tighten the wire stays.

Two distinct sizes of deadeyes have been recovered, implying that both upper and lower masts were in place at the time of her sinking. Indeed, at least one topmast can be seen at the end of her midship mast. While this would seem to indicate that she was under sail at the time, and was not being used as a cargo hulk or barge towed by another vessel, it cannot be a definitive conclusion. Often the lower masts were left in place on such vessels for use in supporting the booms used in loading the vessel's cargo. And on some hulks, several of the sails were left in working order to increase the vessel's stability.

The very full hull lines and the extremely broad, rounded bow of the wreck is quite typical of merchant vessels built in the first half of the nineteenth century. The tonnage rules in force at the time influenced the hull design of these vessels. The formula used to calculate a ship's tonnage, upon which were based its pilot and harbor charges, considered only the vessel's length and beam. No measure of the vessel's depth of hold was considered, so ships were built deep with box-like hull sections to carry the most cargo while incurring the least possible harbor fees. The deep, box-like hull form was carried as far forward as possible to gain the greatest usable cargo space, often resulting in an almost flat-faced bow. Speed was of little consequence since the competition of steamships had not yet arrived. The full hull section and flat bottoms of these ships also permitted them to remain sitting upright in remote harbors, where receding tides often drained the anchorages.

Somewhat similar in design, numerous whaling vessels of the nineteenth century were also built stoutly with very broad, full hulls. Again, speed was of no consequence; whaling voyages commonly lasted up to five years at a time. The main consideration in their design was ample cargo capacity, so her crew could cram as many barrels of the precious whale oil into her hold as possible. Once again, the box-like hull construction had another advantage on such long voyages—the ship could be beached on an outgoing tide if repairs to her hull were necessary.

Indeed, the *Balæna* fits this description to a tee, with her large, box-like hull sitting perfectly upright on the ocean floor. The bow is broad and so flat that, on first encounter, I actually swam along the port side

Numerous deadeyes have been recovered from the Balæna, *both small and large. These indicate that she must have been fully rigged at the time of her sinking. From left to right: Captain George Hoffman, Bob Ehle, Jim Aitkenhead, Jeff Pagano, Tom Packer, Steve Gatto, and, in front, Rick Jaszyn. Photo courtesy of George Hoffman.*

of the ship at sand level, around the bow and started along her starboard side until I suddenly realized that I had changed direction. Only upon retracing my course and carefully examining the hull, did I discover the ship's stem and realize I was looking at her bow!

Her coal cargo, wire stays, and the presence of several mechanical winches on her deck point to the possibility that she survived to see the twilight of the sailing ship. After the introduction of the steamship, the fall of wind-driven craft was inevitable. In order to survive, the operators of sailing ships were forced to cut costs to the barest minimum, which was often achieved by rerigging with fewer sails. With the assistance of a steam-driven donkey winch, the sails could often be handled from the ship's deck, eliminating the need to constantly send men aloft, and thus greatly reducing the vessel's crew requirements. Ironically, coal became a common cargo for these vessels, transported to faraway ports for use by the very steamships that were driving them to extinction.

An exhaustive search through the various shipping registers and other documents for the period of the nineteenth and twentieth centuries turns up a total of six ships bearing the name *Balæna* or *Balaena*. One of these was a huge, steel-hulled steam whaler of 15,715 tons built in 1946 by Harland & Wolff and owned by Hector Whaling, Ltd. of London. She was 555 feet long and can obviously be eliminated in our search for the origin of the sunken ship off the New Jersey coast.

There was a little-known British vessel that was registered at King's Lynn, and had entered the Davis Strait fishery by 1790. Little else is known about this *Balaena,* but it is certain that she is too old to be the ship we are interested in.

Another whaling vessel by this name was built by Dickie Brothers of San Francisco in 1883. She was a wooden-hulled, steam-auxiliary bark of 524 tons and 149 feet in length. Built for the Arctic whale fishery, she was built and fitted in a remarkably short time, sailing on her maiden voyage only three months after her keel was laid. Operated by the Pacific Steam Whaling Company, she sailed on many Arctic voyages in pursuit of the profitable bowhead. During the summer of 1893, the *Balæna* and the *Narwhal* enjoyed the most productive season ever seen in the Arctic fishery, each returning with the bone of over 50 whales. During the 1895 season, the early arrival of winter found the *Balæna* and *Grampus* stranded in the eastern Arctic by advancing pack ice. They managed to find a small harbor to spend the winter in near Cape Parry, Canada, which they named Balaena Bay. The rigors of the Arctic whale fishery had their dangers, however, and on May 1, 1901, the rugged little *Balæna* was lost at St. Lawrence Island in the Bering Sea. Thus she cannot be the *Balæna* we are searching for.

A fourth possibility is a wooden whaling bark named *Balæna,* which was built at New Bedford, Massachusetts, in 1818. She was a small ship, 97 feet long with a 26-foot beam and a registered tonnage of 300. Owned by John Howland, Jr., of New Bedford, she was one of the pioneering vessels that opened up the whaling industry in the Pacific. Under the command of Edmund Gardner of New Bedford, she and the *Equator* of Nantucket share the distinction of being the first whaling vessels to visit the Hawaiian Islands, in September of 1819. Three years later in 1823 Captain Gardner in his little *Balæna* discovered Wake Island in the Pacific.

In 1863 she was sold to H. & S. French of Sag Harbor, New York. This was to be her home port for the remainder of her whaling career. In 1871 she was again sold, this time to John McCullough of New Bedford for the sum of $5,250. Mr. McCullough was the leading local shipbreaker after the Civil War in the New Bedford area: the *Balæna* would not sail on another whaling voyage. Breaking up old wooden ships for scrap was common practice, and this was apparently the fate that befell this adventurous little vessel. The United States Customs Division's *Merchant Vessels of the United States* lists her in both the 1871 and 1872 editions as "Balena [sic] (broken up)." Although her name is misspelled, she is obviously the same vessel since her home port is listed as Sag Harbor, New York, and her tonnage registered as 300.48.

Yet a fifth whale ship named *Balaena* operated out of Bristol, Rhode Island. She was owned by W. H. deWolf and made a South Atlantic voyage from 1832 to 1833. She was registered at 321 tons and was commanded by a Captain Daggett. Nothing more is known about her or her eventual fate.

The sixth and final *Balaena* is the most promising, yet even she is an unlikely candidate. Built in 1872 in Drammen, Norway, by Jorgensen & Knudsen, she was originally named the *Mjolner* and was employed as a sealing vessel. She had a registered tonnage of 416 and was 141 feet long with a 31-foot beam. In 1891 she was bought by R. Kinnes & Company of Dundee, Scotland. Her name was changed to *Balaena*, and she was added to the Dundee register. From here she ventured forth on many whaling voyages, including an expedition to the Antarctic in 1892. She was one of the better known vessels of the Dundee whaling fleet, and was considered quite fast and notoriously lucky. At the outbreak of the First World War, her whaling career ended when she was used by the Hudson's Bay Company to supply munitions to Russia. She was thought to have been lost during a gale in the White Sea on her first voyage in this employ, but this proved untrue.

Although the Balaena *of Dundee represents the most promising candidate for a match with the wreck, there are serious discrepancies with this theory. Photo courtesy of Dundee Art Galleries and Museums.*

Following the war, she was acquired by the Kymo Shipping Company, Ltd., in 1917. She appears in the *Lloyd's Register of Shipping* under this ownership up until the 1933–34 edition, after which both she and the Kymo Shipping Company mysteriously disappear. Further research by Lloyd's, however, indicates that she was sold as a hulk in 1929. The Kymo Shipping Company went into voluntary liquidation on March 8, 1930, being "unable to continue its business by reason of its liabilities." Lloyd's Marine Collection was kind enough to conduct a search of its records for the period 1927–1975, but could find no trace of a vessel by this name sinking anywhere. They are of the opinion that it would have been unlikely for a vessel that was sold as a hulk in 1929 to have been made seaworthy, gone back to sea, and been wrecked off the coast of New Jersey without having been recorded by Lloyd's. They also bring attention to another interesting point: it would have been quite unusual to replace the ship's bell when the vessel was renamed *Balaena.* Thus her bell would have most likely borne her original name, *Mjolner.* This premise is supported by other bells recovered from local wrecks, such as the nearby Dutch freighter *Arundo,* whose recovered bell bore her original name, *Petersfield.* Another example mentioned in this book is the bell from the Chilean freighter *Choapa,* which bore her christened name, *Helga.*

Despite evidence to the contrary, the *Balaena* of Dundee fits the characteristics of our wreck most closely. She was built in 1872, which coincides perfectly with the wreck's wire standing rigging and deadeyes. Perhaps the most convincing evidence is to be found just aft of her mainmast stump, which still rises some 10 to 15 feet vertically above the remains of her deck. Here stands what appears to be the base of an iron smokestack, some 5 feet in diameter, although rising only 6 to 7 feet above the deck. It is deteriorated and filled with rusting iron debris from what must have once been the full height of the stack; yet its form is clear. It appears in exactly the correct location in comparison with the several available photographs of this whale ship. In fact, of all the *Balaena*s that appear in the literature, only the Dundee and San Francisco vessels had steam engines for propulsion (discounting, of course, the huge steel ship built by Harland and Wolff), and the San Francisco ship is known to have foundered in the Bering Sea as mentioned previously.

Yet there are other nagging details that offer evidence to contradict this cursory identification. An important, albeit small, detail is the spelling of the ship's name. On the bell recovered from the wreck, it is spelled out in capital letters with the "AE" diphthong; that is, the two letters are pushed together so that the second vertical of the "A" also forms the spine of the "E"—"Æ." In the photographs of the Dundee ship, however, her name can clearly be seen on both her bow and stern without this peculiarity. *Lloyd's Register* also spells her name without this modification, yet both the New Bedford and San Francisco vessels of the same name appear in the shipping registers with the "AE" in the diphthong format. It seems unlikely that her name

The Balæna's *bell, elegantly engraved with the Latin name for whale, is the only clue to this mysterious vessel's past. Photo by author.*

would have been spelled out in this manner on her bell but not her hull. But what is perhaps the death knell for this identification of the wreck came to light in an attempt to confirm that they were in fact one and the same.

With the help of my friend Dennis Kessler, I used a nylon line to measure the wreck's breadth. Taking the measurement just aft of the smokestack location, I hoped that this measurement, combined with the smokestack's presence, would provide convincing evidence that these were indeed the same ships. Measuring the line we used back on the surface, however, I was vastly disappointed to find it mea-

History of Ships Named Balaena

Vessel	Year built	Rig	Tonnage	Length/Beam/Draft*	Port	Eventual Fate
Balaena	1790	wood, whaleship	—		King's Lynn	unknown
Balaena	1818	wood, whaleship, bark	301 tons	97.2/26.5/13.2	New Bedford Sag Harbor	sold to Sag Harbor, 1863 broken up, 1871
Balaena	1832	wood, whaleship	321 tons	—	Bristol, RI	unknown
Balaena (Mjolner)	1872	wood, steam, auxiliary bark	416 tons	140.9/31.1/16.6	Dundee	sold as hulk, 1929
Balaena	1883	wood, steam auxiliary bark	524 tons	149.5/32.0/17.0	San Francisco	lost at St. Lawrence Island, Bering Sea, May 1, 1901
Balaena	1946	steel, steam whaleship	15715 tons	555.0/77.5/34.5	British	unknown

* dimensions in feet

sured a full 40 feet! While it is possible, perhaps even likely, that her hull would have spread somewhat under the weight of her bellyful of coal over the years, particularly since the measurement we took was not far from where her missing stern section no longer holds her sides together, it seems unlikely that her sides could have spread from her as-built beam of 31 feet to the measured 40 feet of the wreck. The sides of her hull appear quite vertical when viewed from a vantage point on the sand beside her; obviously this would not be the case if her hull had collapsed outward over the years.

Yet if this is not the ship that sits silently on the ocean floor off the New Jersey coast, what vessel is she? If she is not the *Balaena* of Dundee, she is certainly none of the other vessels mentioned here. Was there another, as yet undiscovered, vessel bearing this name? It would seem unlikely that such a large ship could have existed without appearing in any of the shipping registers. There is one other possibility that might fit the evidence at hand. The New Bedford whaleship, whose name appears in several sources with the diphthong spelling, was allegedly broken up in 1871 after being sold "with her inventory, to John McCullough, of New Bedford, for $5,250." After scrapping her, it is likely that her fittings, including her ship's bell, would have been put to some good use. Quite possibly her bell was purchased, perhaps at auction, and put to use on another ship being built at that time. A new ship built in 1871 would undoubtedly have been rigged with wire stays and deadeyes, and quite possibly been fitted with an auxiliary steam engine—much like the Dundee whaler built at this time in Norway. Perhaps the name of the ship sunk off the New Jersey coast was not *Balæna* at all; it may be that she was merely carrying a secondhand bell with its own unique history. This would explain why there is no record of a ship named *Balæna* sinking off this coast, and make the discovery of her real identity nearly impossible.

Perhaps further research will some day turn up records of another ship named *Balæna* that better fits the description of the wreck. Or, perhaps, something will be recovered from her grave site far below the Atlantic swells that will yield a further clue to her history. Until then we can only speculate as to her true identity, her demise, and the fate of her crew. We have a ship, and we have a name. Yet we cannot even say with certainty that the two belong together. But locked deep within the very soul of that handsome bronze bell is the unique history of a ship that was once christened with the Latin name for the great and noble whale: *Balæna.*

A Dive

on the

USS *Wilkes-Barre*

———

———

———

———

———

———

———

———

———

———

———

———

———

———

———

———

Near the southernmost point in the United States, there lies a great warship, all but forgotten by most in this time of relative peace. Though still and impotent now, she once fought gallantly for the world's freedom in World War II. The Cleveland-class light cruiser USS *Wilkes-Barre* lies beneath 250 feet of water, some seven miles south of Saddlebunch Key in Florida's southward-reaching island chain. The challenge of diving her rusting hulk calls to those who are fascinated by such adventures, and those who answer her call are well rewarded. To see her solemn silhouette on silent patrol deep beneath the waters she once sailed is to fall in love with her.

Five of us had made the journey south to dive the wreck, something for which we had been trying to find the time over the past several years. The wreck had whispered its siren call even over the vast distance separating us. Wreck divers are a close-knit group, and word had filtered quietly northward until the *Wilkes-Barre* had become almost legendary. She was a formidable challenge, lying in deep water and often frequented by strong currents. All five of us were experienced in deep, decompression diving in the cold northern waters of New Jersey and Long Island, and we were veterans of several trips to the famed Italian luxury liner *Andrea Doria*. But these were unfamiliar waters, compelling us to proceed with caution.

Since this was a very deep dive, we had come south with special recommendations from Captain Steve Bielenda, who runs the dive charter boat R/V *Wahoo* out of Captree, New York. He is a personal friend of Captain Billy Deans, who was kind enough to take us to this magnificent wreck in mid-February, not prime weather for the region. Thanks to his friendship with Captain Bielenda, Captain Billy allowed us to make this deep, difficult dive without first checking us out on a shallower dive site, something he does not normally do.

Captain Billy proved to be an excellent host. He is enthusiastic, knowledgeable, and extremely safety conscious, as well as an excellent diver and boat captain. The man has seemingly boundless energy, and he has pioneered diving on the *Wilkes-Barre*. His entire operation, and particularly the special system he uses for diving this

The Cleveland-class light cruiser U.S.S. Wilkes-Barre *served her country well during the struggle against Japanese imperialism during World War II. Following the war she was placed in mothballs until January 15, 1971, when she was struck from the Navy list. Photo courtesy of the Underwater Explosive Research Division, U.S. Navy.*

wreck, is built around the premise that safety comes first, and he practices what he preaches.

———

———

The USS *Wilkes-Barre* was built in 1943 at Camden, New Jersey, by the New York Shipbuilding Corporation. At 610-feet long with a top speed of 33 knots, she was a powerful and fleet-footed addition to our naval forces in the Pacific. Named after the city of Wilkes-Barre, Pennsylvania, she was quite an active participant in World War II. After commissioning and fitting out, she embarked upon a shakedown cruise in Chesapeake Bay and the British West Indies before proceeding to the Pacific via the Panama Canal.

Designated a test target, the Wilkes-Barre *was towed to Key West, Florida, where she was instrumented and subjected to a series of underwater explosions. Photo courtesy of the Underwater Explosive Research Division, U.S. Navy.*

Arriving at Ulithi, Caroline Islands, on December 14, 1944, she soon began her active participation in the war, which would go on virtually nonstop until the final victory was achieved. Her first taste of action came in support of carrier air strikes against various targets on Formosa, Ryukus, and Luzon, and along the Chinese coast. These actions took place throughout most of January 1945. At one point the cruiser was forced to ride out a two-day gale in the South China Sea. With heavy seas and strong winds coming out of the northeast, she

On May 12, 1972, the Wilkes-Barre *finally succumbed to the bombard-ment of explosive tests and cracked in half. Shortly thereafter she settled to the ocean bottom 250 feet below. Photo courtesy of the Underwater Explosive Research Division, U.S. Navy.*

reportedly rolled as much as 38 degrees, surely testing the constitu-tions of even the most iron-stomached sailors.

In mid-February, 1945, the *Wilkes-Barre* helped screen the fleet's carriers from air attack during a diversionary raid on Tokyo. This bombing of the Japanese mainland, the first since Lieutenant Colonel

Doolittle's "Tokyo Raiders" in April 1942, was a cover for the important invasion of Iwo Jima taking place simultaneously to the south. After two days of air strikes on Tokyo, the diversionary force headed south to assist in the real operation at Iwo Jima. On February 21 and 22, the *Wilkes-Barre*'s 6-inch guns were called upon to assist in the shore bombardment of the island. By day, the cruiser's Kingfisher aircraft directed her gunfire, helping to ensure the destruction of various enemy positions. Her assistance was praised by the marines on the beach, who commended her prompt and accurate fire and credited her for turning back a strong Japanese counterattack during the night.

On April 1, 1945, American forces began what would prove to be one of the most difficult amphibious operations undertaken during the Pacific War: the invasion of Okinawa. Once again, the *Wilkes-Barre* was there to lend her support. Throughout the month of April, the *Wilkes-Barre* and her sister cruisers protected the carriers, which themselves were providing air support for the operation, from enemy aircraft. The *Wilkes-Barre*'s barrage of antiaircraft fire was credited with downing five Japanese aircraft and assisting in the destruction of three more. The operation continued throughout the month of May, and the *Wilkes-Barre* tallied up two more enemy aircraft to her credit. On many occasions, the cruiser's own aircraft crews braved hazardous conditions to rescue downed carrier pilots and, in one case, were awarded Air Medals for their work.

Undoubtedly the most dramatic episode of her war career occurred early on the morning of May 11, when two kamikazes dove out of the sky and impaled themselves upon the broad deck of the fleet carrier USS *Bunker Hill,* causing her to erupt in flames. The *Wilkes-Barre* was ordered alongside the stricken carrier to render assistance. The cruiser's commander brought his ship so close to the carrier that the *Bunker Hill*'s overhanging 40-mm gun emplacements struck and damaged the *Wilkes-Barre* while she brought ten streams of water to bear on the ravaging flames. Forty men were rescued from the burning carrier before the *Wilkes-Barre* was forced to back off a short distance. Here she rigged a breeches buoy and evacuated another 61 injured sailors. She remained faithfully alongside, assisting with the fire fighting until the flames were well under control. The *Bunker Hill's* captain later commended the crew of the *Wilkes-Barre* for their valiant assistance in saving the carrier from the ravenous flames that engulfed her.

After the dropping of the two atomic bombs and Japan's surrender, the *Wilkes-Barre* formed part of the Third Fleet entering Tokyo Bay to cover the demilitarization of Japan. She spent the remainder of 1945 carrying out occupation duties in Japan and China, including the seizure of two former Japanese midget submarine bases. In January of 1946, the well-worn cruiser finally set sail for home, arriving in Philadelphia in March via Pearl Harbor, San Pedro, California, and the Panama Canal. She remained in service, performing light peacetime duties, including a 1946 goodwill cruise to Europe, until October 9, 1947, when she was decommissioned and placed in mothballs at Philadelphia. Here she remained for nearly 25 years, quietly awaiting the call to duty.

On January 15, 1971, she was struck from the Navy list, having been declared "not essential to the defense of the United States." However, she had one last duty to perform for her country. Taken to Key West, Florida, she was heavily instrumented and subjected to underwater explosive tests. The data obtained during her destruction hopefully will help future generations of warships to better withstand the effects of underwater explosives. On May 12, 1972, her 610-foot hulk was broken neatly in two just forward of her afterstack. The stern section sank of its own accord shortly thereafter, settling on an even keel on the sandy bottom. The bow section required a scuttling charge the following day to complete the job. It is here that she found her final resting place, beneath 250 feet of clear, blue water in southern Florida.

The owner of this distinguished service record was the object of our quest. We had come to explore her, to photograph her, but mostly just to marvel at her pristine form resting quietly on the bottom, far below the waves she once proudly plowed.

Upon arriving in Key West and checking into our hotel, we stopped in at Key West Diver, the dive shop owned and operated by Captain Billy Deans. It was quite windy during our drive through the Florida Keys and, in offshore diving, windy translates into rough seas and the possibility of our charter being cancelled. After talking to Captain Billy, however, we found that the next day was supposed to be beautiful, even better than we could have hoped for in mid-February. But now a new concern had arisen; he was worried that there would be strong currents on the wreck, making diving impossible. Had we driven 1500 miles for nothing? We had only three days in which to make the dive, after which Billy had prior obligations, and we had to return to New York and our own individual livelihoods.

The following dawn brought a bright, sunny, and warm day with only the slightest of breezes—a fine beginning for a day of diving in the open ocean. As Captain Billy topped off our scuba tanks to ensure that we had plenty of air for this deep dive, he again expressed his concern about the possibility of strong currents. There was no way of foretelling this, however, and we would have to await our arrival at the wreck site to see whether we could make the dive. So we pressed on with the business at hand, loading heavy air tanks, a large oxygen cylinder for decompression, camera equipment, dive suits, and assorted gear onto Billy's boat *Key West Diver*.

Leaving the dock, we threaded our way through a narrow passage of mangroves and out into the channel leading to the open ocean. The ride out to "the Barre," as she is affectionately called, took about one hour. We marveled at the clarity of the water, gazing down through it and watching the sandy bottom rush by at high speed as we enjoyed the bright Florida sunshine.

Guided to the vicinity of the wreck site by loran, we were again surprised by the strange methods used in these southern waters. Utilizing the loran set and chart recorder to locate the wreck, Captain Billy motored about looking for his mooring buoy from atop the small tuna tower on his boat. The amazing part of this procedure is

Captain Billy Deans pauses next to one of the Wilkes-Barre's *coral-encrusted 20-mm antiaircraft guns. The barrels are missing from all the small-calibre guns on board the ship. Photo by author.*

that the mooring buoy is normally located some 40 feet below the surface, and it is usually found with ease just by looking down through the crystal clear water! Such a procedure would be preposterous up North due to the generally murky water found there. Unfortunately the mooring buoy had been sunk since its last use. This was merely an inconvenience—as Billy and his crew member Eric combined their efforts to set up a temporary mooring to use for the next several days. There appeared to be no appreciable current, and all our previous fears and worries were immediately relieved.

Dennis Kessler and I were to make the first descent to the wreck, followed shortly thereafter by the second team of Pete Guglieri, Gene Howley, and Ed Murphy. Once the mooring was set and we were geared up, Dennis and I rolled off the stern of the boat and swam to the bow where the mooring line was waiting to guide us to the wreck below.

––––––

––––––

As we begin our descent through the crystal clear Gulf Stream waters, a vast army of barracuda appear below us. They hover motionless, aligned in ranks about the mooring line. As we approach, they silently part to allow our passage, but quickly close above us as if to challenge our return to the surface.

The vertical visibility is fantastic, enabling us to see some 100 feet of mooring line stretched out before us. A few curious barracuda follow us downward, but our minds are concentrating on what will soon appear below us and we pay them no heed. As we descend ever downward, the visibility drops slightly as a faint haze becomes apparent in the distance, but still the water is exceptionally clear. What begins as a faint shadow evident in the depths below quickly takes the shape of a huge smokestack at the end of the thin line we have been following since leaving the surface. The sun is shining brightly up above, and its rays reach down even to this great depth to illuminate the scene before us. Landing atop the stack, I glance quickly at my depth gauge to see that we have reached a depth of 145 feet. Dropping off the forward side of the stack, we come upon a set of huge searchlights, one on either side of the ship. Each points outward from its own small platform high above the ship's deck, still searching for some target to illuminate. One still retains broken fragments of its great lens, even after the powerful explosions that wracked her hull during her destruction. These two searchlights mark the forward-most portion of the superstructure found on the stern section of the wreck.

Turning toward the stern, we begin to swim aft against a slight current running over the otherwise still ship. Just astern of the

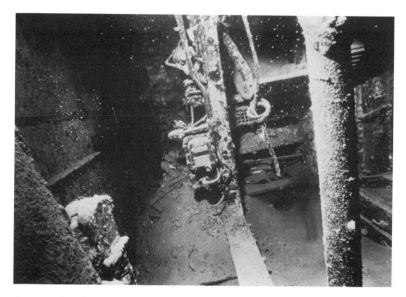

An open hatch gives access to the cramped interior of the 5-inch gun turret. Entering such cramped compartments, particularly at the great depth at which the Wilkes-Barre lies, can be hazardous and should be attempted only with extreme caution. Photo by author.

smokestack, lie two port-and-starboard twin 20-mm antiaircraft emplacements. They are complete except for the gun barrels, which are missing from all of the antiaircraft guns on board. This small mystery is solved later after talking to Captain Billy, who explains that the gun barrels were stored inside the ship's superstructure on racks, ironically to protect them from the salt air. Covered in red and green coral, the barrel-less guns stare helplessly out into the blue void, unable to defend the ship against the marauding barracuda and grouper as they once did so successfully against enemy aircraft. Glancing downward, I catch sight of a more serious set of guns. Dropping from my perch high in the superstructure, I descend to examine a twin 5-inch gun turret. Pointing forward they appear almost ready to fire, looking none the worse for their 16 years of

The ship's fire control rooms were her combat centers, enabling her crew to accurately aim the destructive power of her potent guns. Photo by author.

The interior of the ship's aft fire control room is a fascinating place, especially with its abundance of artifacts waiting to be recovered. Intact radios, gauges, and radar consoles stand just as they did on the day she sank. Photo by author.

submergence. Examining the great barrels, I ponder both their historic past and their present idle existence here on the bottom. How many times were they fired, both in war and in peace? What destruction did they bring to their adversaries, and what great victories to the men whose very lives depended upon them?

Swimming aft I come across an open doorway leading into the interior of the ship. I cannot resist the temptation to venture inside this stately vessel, and I enter her cautiously. The room is a jumbled but recognizable remnant of its former self. Light fixtures still hang from overhead, unable to light the interior, a task momentarily accomplished by my dive light. As my light sweeps slowly across the room, I see a vast array of debris. Counters and workbenches run along several walls, their drawers spilling haphazardly onto the

A lone barracuda flashes past one of the many 20-mm antiaircraft emplacements found on the warship. Photo by author.

Deep inside her cavernous interior, the missing small-calibre gun barrels can be found hanging in racks where they were once protected from the corrosive salt air. Photo by author.

floor. Some of the portholes have been removed by divers, and only the storm covers are left hanging motionless on their hinges, allowing a faint glow of exterior light to penetrate the darkness inside. In one corner stands a chair, the seat springs all that remain of its cushioning. Against the far wall hangs a large sink, now badly in need of cleaning. Assorted items lie jumbled in a heap in the center of the room. Everything here is covered with a thin film of fine, white silt, giving the appearance that a long-neglected dusting is in order. The interior is fascinating but time is short at these depths, and I must press on with my underwater tour.

Swimming out through the doorway I entered a few short minutes ago, I swim aft on the main deck. A quick glance at my gauges tells me that my air supply is one-third gone. Moving on toward the stern, I come to the after end of the ship's superstructure where I am

One of the ship's 40-mm antiaircraft guns, minus its gun barrels. Photo by author.

compelled to stop. Standing on the main deck at a depth of 210 feet, I gaze up in awe at the two after 6-inch gun turrets towering overhead, dwarfing all other sights I have seen here. Their sheer size is hypnotic, their massive silhouette framed by a backdrop of the ever-present barracuda. I swim slowly upward and aft to the lower of the two turrets, barely noticing that the main deck is cracked and sagging, evidence of structural damage sustained by the ship during her sinking. Landing atop the after turret, I find myself staring into the muzzles of the powerful 6-inch guns of the adjacent turret. Although covered with nearly two decades of marine growth, the rifling is still clearly visible within the barrels. I pause here, wishing I could freeze time and ponder this scene at length. Time is never stagnant, however, and I can linger no longer. With a parting glance at her guns, I drop back to the main deck and swim forward along the starboard side of the ship's superstructure.

I pass many doorways, some open and some tightly shut, all beckoning to be explored on some future dive. Moving quickly up a stairway to the next higher deck, I pass more antiaircraft guns and hatchways and a 5-inch gun turret. I finally find myself at the smokestack and the mooring line waiting to guide me back to the surface. I ascend slowly up the line, hand over hand, gazing steadily downward, savoring every last second as this magnificent ship fades slowly from view.

We hang onto the mooring line a few feet below the surface for nearly an hour of decompression, alternately breathing air and pure oxygen to speed the elimination of absorbed nitrogen from our bodies. I stare emptily at the vast army of barracuda hovering motionless around us; my mind wanders as I find myself filled with both admiration and jealousy at the ease with which they exist in this liquid world. Thinking about the dive, I relive over and over again my experiences on the great warship sitting silently on the ocean floor.

The *Wilkes-Barre* still retains her dignity, and is more than willing to share her world with those few who take the challenge. For a few fleeting moments we were permitted a rare and awe-inspiring glimpse of this great warship. While the moment passed quickly, the memories will always remain, and with them the longing to return and see her once again.

The
Tragic Fate
of the
SS *Suffolk*

———
———
———
———
———
———
———
———
———
———
———
———
———
———
———

Gliding slowly out of Lake Montauk, New York, at 5:30 A.M., we are greeted by a peaceful, flat calm sea. The early morning silence is broken only by the rumble of the research vessel *Wahoo*'s diesel engines pushing us out past Montauk Point and into the open ocean. The flat sea and bright morning sunlight promise a pleasant trip offshore and a fine day of diving on yet another new and unexplored shipwreck. Our only problem will be locating the remains of the unlucky vessel.

The United States Coast Guard is threatening to shut down one of its five loran transmitters this morning for maintenance. Theoretically, we should be able to find the wreck with the remaining operational loran signals. However, we have never visited this particular wreck site and are not sure the loran coordinates that we have been given are accurate. We want the best chance of finding her and, unfortunately, that chance rests with the transmitter that the Coast Guard is planning to shut down on this, of all mornings.

All on board begin to wonder if we will be able to find our quarry. I find myself overcome by a bizarre feeling of deja vu. Several years earlier a similar attempt to visit the remains of the SS *Suffolk* had been foiled by identical loran problems. The memories of that ill-fated trip fill my head as we once again head out to the wreck site, amidst an air of uncertainty.

A December Gale

The tragic story of the demise of the collier *Suffolk* begins in late 1943, in the midst of the Second World War. The tired, old ship was doing her part to support the Allied war effort when she departed Newport News, Virginia, on December 9, headed for Boston with 6798 tons of bituminous coal. The 32-year-old steamship found herself involved in the second war of her career. She had been built by the New York Shipbuilding Company back in 1911 at Camden, New Jersey, and had served her country well during the Great War. Though an

An old and weary coastal collier, the SS Suffolk *saw service during both world wars. Photo by John L. Lochhead, courtesy of The Mariners' Museum, Newport News, Virginia.*

unimposing 365 feet long and 4607 gross tons, she was a workhorse as her long career indicates. Nevertheless, such an ancient vessel must be expected to show signs of her age, and the *Suffolk* was no exception. Only one month earlier, a 2-inch hole and a section of badly deteriorated hull plates had been discovered 6 feet below her deep-load water line. The damage was temporarily repaired in Newport News by welding a 2-foot by 4-foot steel plate to the outside of her hull over the damaged area. After just one voyage up the coast to Boston, however, leakage was discovered around the edges of the patch, and a new and larger plate was welded into place. And at the time of her last annual Coast Guard inspection, on July 26, an extensive ten-page list of modifications and repairs to the aging vessel was completed. Nevertheless, Captain Charles Thistle and Chief Engineer Irving Bennett had the utmost confidence in their ship, often referring to her as a "good old job."

The weather forecast for the New York area for December 11 was unpleasant, but unalarming. Slightly colder and somewhat windy weather promised to bring more seasonable conditions to the eastern seaboard, which had been experiencing a mild winter to date. Snow flurries were expected as well. But on the day of sailing, the weather was quite mild, with the winds variable and averaging only 7.4 miles per hour. At the last minute a replacement crewman had to be found; an oiler, William Bennett, Jr., quit the ship to join the crew of another vessel, the SS *Jonathan Edwards*. He was quickly replaced by a Mr. Nick Nelson, who signed on the official United States Coast Guard Crew List in the 37th spot, listing himself as hailing from Newport News, and having no next of kin. As events would unfold, Mr. Bennett's decision to leave the crew of the *Suffolk* would prove to be the most fortunate choice of his life. At 11:45 A.M., the SS *Suffolk* set sail, bound for her home port of Boston, Massachusetts.

Friday, December 10, found the *Suffolk* plying steadily northward along the New Jersey coastline. A fresh southwest breeze and a steady barometer reading of 30.00 inches of mercury provided no warning of what was in store for the next 24 hours. About 5 P.M., off Barnegat, New Jersey, she passed within sight of the collier SS *James Ellwood Jones*, owned by the Pocahontas Steamship Company and commanded by Captain M. White. The *Jones* had left the same Virginia port four hours after the *Suffolk*. Captain White would later tell an inquiry board that the *Suffolk* "showed no exceptional list and seemed to have normal freeboard" when he sighted her. As fate would have it, the crew of the *Jones* would be the last to set eyes upon the doomed Boston collier.

Nature is an untamed and often unpredictable entity, and early on the morning of December 11, the mild spell of weather came to a violent and abrupt end. The temperature dropped rapidly, reportedly falling 22 degrees in a span of nine hours as an icy gale struck the New York region. The winds were clocked at upwards of 72 miles per hour out of the northwest—barely short of hurricane force. In New York City, store windows were smashed and trees uprooted; women were knocked down by the violent gusts, and pedestrians were cut by flying glass from shattered plate-glass windows. In Upper New York Bay an 8000-ton Liberty ship was driven aground, while a Navy patrol launch was sunk in the Lower Bay. At La

Guardia Field, a commercial airliner carrying 18 passengers was bounced 50 feet off the runway by the furious wind while attempting to land! In New Britain, Connecticut, the roof was ripped off a 4-story, 16-family brick apartment house by the ferocious gale-force winds. The cold temperatures were especially unwelcome, with New York in the midst of a coal shortage.

If the gale could wreak such havoc on land, the conditions far at sea on the unsheltered ocean must have been unimaginable. Yet far offshore, miles from any safe refuge, was where the 37 crewmen aboard the ancient collier *Suffolk* found themselves when the raging gale struck. Also on board the doomed vessel was a six-man naval gun crew, along to defend her against the marauding German U-boats, which had already claimed an alarming number of vessels off the American coast. But the gun crew could do nothing to defend the ship against the furious storm in which she now found herself.

The route to Boston Harbor had taken the small ship far offshore to clear Montauk Point at the eastern end of Long Island. It was here that the fate of the *Suffolk* was to be decided. The old ship and her crew must have battled hard against the mountainous seas driven by the near hurricane-force winds. She had survived countless storms before this and had withstood the onslaught of the German grey wolves of two world wars. Doubtless her crew, though frightened by the incredible seas they faced, fought to the end to survive. But the violent forces of nature are sometimes insurmountable, and the weary old collier could no longer sustain her fight for survival.

At 11:43 A.M. the first distress signal was sent by wireless. Radio Amagansett (WSL) intercepted a message from the *Suffolk* (KGGN):

SOS DE KGGN POSITION 7158 W 4043 N WE ARE LISTING HEAVILY NEED HELP

The message was quickly repeated at 11:46 A.M.:

SOS DE KGGN WE ARE LISTING HEAVY WE UR-GENTLY NEED HELP POSITION 7158 WEST 4043 NORTH

Less than a half hour later, at 12:03 P.M., the last desperate communication from the crew of the *Suffolk* was received:

SOS SOS DE KGGN WE ARE FOUNDERING WE
NEED HELP IMMEDIATELY AR DE KGGN BT 111603

These brief messages were the last ever heard from the brave crew of the Boston collier.

Shortly after the distress signals were received, a massive rescue operation was begun. At 12:16 the Eastern Sea Frontier (ESF) ordered five U.S. Navy destroyer escorts, the USS *Scott, Burke, Weber, Schmitt,* and *Frament* to the *Suffolk*'s reported position. But their location placed them 64 miles east of where the foundering collier lay; it would be hours before they could reach the *Suffolk.* The Navy destroyer USS *Semmes,* as well as the tugs *Kewaydin, Falcon,* and *Fire Island,* were also dispatched to the scene to aid in the hunt for the stricken ship.

At 4:30 P.M., the USS *Scott* wirelessed that the group of destroyer escorts was making every effort to reach the *Suffolk*'s position. She reported that the ships were fighting severe sea and ice conditions, and that she herself had suffered a ruptured deck plate forward, and might be forced to slow down. She estimated that she was making good a speed of only about 9 knots, and was still 42 miles from the *Suffolk.* The USS *Semmes* reported in at 9:00 P.M.; since 3:00 P.M. she had been in the area downwind of the position given in the distress call but had sighted nothing.

The search continued into the night, and at 2:45 A.M. on the morning of December 12, the USS *Scott* again radioed to report her progress. She advised that she had searched upwind toward the *Suffolk*'s position for a distance of 40 miles with a 15-mile scouting line. Though their nighttime search was aided by bright moonlight, they could find no trace of the collier or her crew. She turned southwestward and continued the search downwind. Two hours later, at 4:21 A.M., the destroyer escorts were ordered to New York. The USS *Semmes* and the tugs *Falcon, Kewaydin,* and *Fire Island* remained to search for some sign of wreckage or survivors.

The Suffolk *was lost in a raging gale off Montauk, Long Island, on December 11, 1943. None of her crew survived to tell of their ordeal. Drawing by author.*

At 4:24 A.M. the Ditch Plains Life Boat Station near Montauk on Long Island's south shore reported that a patrolman had sighted three red flares at approximately 40° 51' 40" N, 71° 41' W. A second patrolman reported that he had also seen something at about the same time, but thought that it was a star. The search vessels were promptly advised of the sighting, but the USS *Semmes* relayed the opinion that the patrolmen might have seen the red filters employed on the destroyer escorts' searchlights. The first patrolman was persistent, however, claiming that the flares appeared orange as they rose up from the sea, lasted several seconds, and then changed color to red as they fell.

Throughout December 12 and 13, the search for the crew of the missing collier continued. During the day, both aircraft and blimps assisted in the hunt, while at night the destroyer and the three tugs continued the search alone. But all efforts to locate any sign of the vessel proved fruitless. Finally, at 5:40 P.M. on December 13 all hope was given up; the search for the SS *Suffolk* was called to a halt. After an intensive 52-hour search involving nine surface vessels, aircraft, and even a blimp, absolutely no trace of wreckage or survivors could be found. The *Suffolk* had vanished without a trace and was presumed lost with all hands.

Eighteen days later on December 31, the destroyer escort USS *Reeves* found a life raft containing two bodies in position 38° 19' N, 65° 28' W. The equipment found on board the raft along with the papers discovered on the bodies established that they were from the SS *Suffolk*. The medical officer aboard the *Reeves* examined the bodies and reported that they had died of exposure at least two days prior. The deceased, Bobby Joe Anderson of Dallas, Texas, and William Allen Anderson of the U.S. Naval Reserve were buried at sea, and the life raft in which they were found was sunk. These were the only bodies ever recovered.

The life raft was found 320 miles southeast of Montauk Point; it had drifted over 300 miles in 20 days. If these two men had survived, they would have told an incredible tale of survival, having spent 20 days in an open boat in the wintery North Atlantic. But destiny had other plans for these brave men, and along with them died their incredible story of battle against the cruel sea. The world will never know the extent of their suffering at the hands of this terrible storm.

Eleven days after the tragic sinking, on December 22, a Navy rescue tug made contact with a stationary metal target at location 40° 52.8' N, 71° 13.2' W. The tug mounted a depth-charge attack, suspecting the object was a submarine contact. The attack brought up wreckage with no marine growth on it, and it was concluded that this object on the ocean floor must be the remains of the SS *Suffolk*. This is the location at which the post-war wreck charts placed the ship. This position is 35 miles east of the position given by the ship's crew in their distress signal. Is it possible that the vessel drifted this far before finally disappearing beneath the tremendous waves? Or was the radioed position merely in error, due to the strain on the crew caused by the gale? The answer to this question along with a myriad of others will never be known.

Towering mutely over the remains of the steamship Suffolk, *the ship's huge propeller forms a lonely memorial to her brave crew who lost their lives in a winter gale off Montauk, New York, during World War II. Is her missing rudder perhaps a clue to the cause of her foundering? Photo by author.*

An Inquiry Board was convened at the Office of the District Coast Guard Officer, Fifth Naval District in Norfolk, Virginia. A thorough investigation was conducted in an attempt to determine the cause of the sinking. The Board concentrated mainly on the aspects of the vessel's seaworthiness and the loading of her cargo in the Virginia port prior to her final voyage. After reviewing various documents and interviewing several witnesses about the loading of her cargo, it was concluded that the vessel was properly manned and seaworthy, and that her cargo was properly loaded with virtually no possibility of having shifted. She was, however, heavily loaded at the time, with approximately 95 percent of her available cargo space filled. This was common practice during the war, since the shipping industry attempted to compensate for numerous inevitable delays in port by loading their ships to maximum capacity. At the time of the *Suffolk*'s foundering, there was a strong wind out of the northwest blowing at approximately 60 miles per hour, accompanied by a heavy sea and freezing temperatures. The *Suffolk* had adequate boatage and rafts with two metal lifeboats, four life rafts, and two balsa floats.

Due to the lack of survivors and any concrete evidence as to what actually happened to the vessel, the Inquiry Board's conclusions were necessarily based on assumptions, as well as what little evidence they did have:

> The conditions evident, however, indicate that due to a
> combination of circumstances, namely: strong winds of gale
> force, heavy sea, below freezing temperature, considerable
> quantities of water turning to ice with the attendant ten-
> dency to block the free passage of water through the freeing
> ports [scuppers], resulted in placing a tremendous addi-
> tional weight on the vessel, and reduced the reserve buoy-
> ancy to a point where remaining afloat was no longer
> possible; that most of the ship's superstructure and rigging
> would have been covered by ice. . . Therefore, the only
> possible conclusion at which this Board can arrive is that the
> SS *Suffolk* foundered under the increased and uncontrollable
> weight brought about as above stated.

Just forward of the propeller, the hull is broken open. Inside her engine room stands a gong bell, which last rang almost fifty years ago. Was its last ring to signal the abandonment of the tired old vessel in the height of the December gale which sank her? Photo by author.

Thus concluded the investigation into the loss of the SS *Suffolk*; the insatiable sea had once again thoughtlessly swallowed up another of man's frail ships, without leaving so much as a clue to the events of her last hours. For most of the world, it was but one more loss in a string of hardships brought about by the war in Europe. But for those left behind by the 43 men lost in the tragedy, the world was a changed place.

Two-and-one-half months after the ship foundered, the wife of the vessel's second mate, Joseph H. Wagg, Jr., wrote a letter to the U.S. Coast Guard. Mrs. Mary Wagg inquired if any more information about the final fate of the ship and her crew had come to light. Even at this late date, she held out hope that somehow her husband or some of the crew might have miraculously survived; perhaps they were rescued by some passing ship and taken to a foreign port. The letter is sad reading. Mrs. Wagg was pregnant and expecting shortly, and she desperately asked for some favorable news about her beloved husband. The tragic sinking of the small steamship had consequences that reached beyond the 43 brave men who lost their lives in the December gale.

Hanging just above the gong bell, this gauge panel once informed the Suffolk's *crew of the status of the ship's engines and boilers. Photo by author.*

Epilogue

———

Diving the wreck proved to be an eerie experience after studying the terrible drama and somber loss of life interwoven into the story of her sinking. The water surrounding the *Suffolk* is deep and clear, though somewhat dark as the silty-grey ocean floor partially absorbs what little sunlight reaches the bottom. The *Suffolk* herself lies largely intact, though completely upside down, 180 feet below the ocean's surface. The middle section of her hull is broken and twisted, largely unrecognizable in form. This is, perhaps, a result of the depth-charge attack mounted by the salvage tug that discovered the wreck, 11 days after her last SOS message. Alternatively, it may be the result of the merciless sea's final onslaught, breaking her fragile hull in two at the moment of her surrender. Aft, the hull regains its rightful form, and at the extreme stern of the old vessel, a diver is greeted by a magnificent sight. The huge four-bladed propeller towers mutely over the remains of the small collier; it is a picturesque scene as her intact keel runs straight and true toward the bow of the vessel. The ship at this point appears to be in perfect condition, save her missing rudder and strange orientation on the bottom. Was this perhaps the cause of her foundering? Was her huge rudder torn away by the mountainous seas during the icy gale? If she indeed lost her steering gear, the *Suffolk* would have found herself helpless and out of control, completely at the mercy of the cruel North Atlantic storm.

Perhaps this was when the crew took to the lifeboats, knowing their ship was doomed. If so, they must have already known their own fate as they struggled in the numbing cold, fighting the ferocious wind and sea and ice in order to abandon the foundering collier and entrust their lives to the small, frail lifeboats that were their only remaining hope for survival.

War

Cruise

of

the

U-123

———
———
———
———
———
———
———
———
———
———
———
———

August 21, 1987, 2:00 A.M.:

The wind has picked up quite a bit, causing a 3- to 4-foot sea to keep the dive boat *Wahoo* in a state of perpetual motion. Sleep is elusive; the incessant rocking of a boat in the open ocean always makes sleeping nearly impossible for me. The movement pauses every few minutes like clockwork, as if to tease the intended sleeper with a momentary peaceful calm and the prospect of much-needed slumber, only to begin anew and dash the illusion once again.

My attempts at slumber futile, I rise and wander out on deck. The night is dark and incredibly clear. On this otherwise still night, the only sound to be heard is the low rumble of the boat's generator. Stars abound everywhere in the night sky, and I find myself once again overcome by the miraculous quantity of heavenly bodies visible so far from the distracting lights of civilization. Yet, even here, some 30 miles off the Long Island coastline, a glow on the western horizon is clearly visible evidence of our proximity to the city of New York. It seems incredible that this light can be seen more than seventy miles east of Manhattan! But the sky overhead is dark, and I can make out the tiny cluster of light that is the Pleiades to the east, while Cassiopeia looms high overhead, watching all below her. The Big Dipper sits low on the horizon to the north, pointing upward, ever-reaching toward the pole star that served the ancient mariners so well.

My mind drifts back in time to the events that occurred here 45 years ago and are the reason for our presence here. We are anchored over the hulk of the British tanker *Coimbra,* only the second ship to be torpedoed by the submarines of the German Kriegsmarine off the American coast during the second of the world wars. We have come to explore her time-worn remains, for she offers a window into the past and a view of her own unique place in history. Gazing toward the faint light in the western sky, we see why the German submariners returned from their first American patrols referring to this coast as the "Happy Hunting Grounds." Silhouetted against the brightly lit shoreline, merchant ships were literally "sitting ducks." The glow on the horizon tonight evokes a strong link to the past. Lieutenant

Reinhard Hardegen, in command of the *U-123*, wrote about the many lights of the New York suburbs in his logbook, scant hours before he happened upon the British tanker *Coimbra* and made her his second victim of Operation "Paukenschlag."

Operation "Paukenschlag"

The declaration of war by Germany on the United States on December 11, 1941, found American coastal defenses quite unprepared for the coming conflict with the German U-boats. War with Germany came only four days after the attack by the Japanese on Pearl Harbor, and the submarine menace was perhaps overshadowed by the violent drama that had unfolded in the Pacific. Germany's declaration of war seemed to have no immediate effect on shipping along the eastern seaboard—in fact, life went on much as usual. The war seemed far away, and coastal cities remained brightly lit throughout the night. Ships continued to display their navigation lights; coastal aids to navigation, such as lighthouses and lightships, remained in operation. Wireless traffic proceeded uninhibited.

In Germany, however, the fact that America was now a participant in the war did not want for attention. Immediate plans were made by Admiral Karl Doenitz, Commander in Chief of the U-boat branch of the German Navy, to send a fleet of *unterseeboots* to operate in American waters. Due to other German commitments, all that could be spared for the campaign were five submarines. The operation received the code designation "Paukenschlag," which translates as "a beating of kettledrums." The five boats were to operate in unison off the American coast from the St. Lawrence to Cape Hatteras, forming a carefully planned and coordinated surprise attack—a blow to the unprepared and unsuspecting coastal defenses of the new enemy. The first of the submarines left for the far side of the Atlantic during the third week in December, only days after America's entry into the war.

The five boats chosen to participate in the operation were: *U-66* under Commander Richard Zapp, *U-109* under Lieutenant Heinrich Bleichrodt, *U-123* under Lieutenant Reinhard Hardegen, *U-125* under Lieutenant Ulrich Folkers, and *U-130* under Commander Ernst Kals. The submarine commanders were under strict orders not to attack any shipping under 10,000 tons until they received a signal from Doenitz that the operation was to begin. Doenitz wanted the element of surprise on his side, and any premature attacks were sure to warn the Americans of the coming onslaught. As each of the boats neared the American coast, their crews anxiously awaited the signal from Admiral Doenitz. On January 9 the wireless message finally came: Operation "Paukenschlag" was to begin on January 13.

Aboard the type IXB boat *U-123*, the crew knew good hunting lay ahead when they were informed of their patrol area: the target-rich area outside New York Harbor! Perhaps the excitement of the impending hunt, which must have filled the small submarine, is explanation enough for Lieutenant Hardegen's premature trigger finger. The ambitious skipper couldn't resist temptation when the

British passenger steamer *Cyclops* crossed his path a full two days before the scheduled start of "Paukenschlag." Sailing alone 300 miles east of Cape Cod, the *Cyclops* with a tonnage of 9076 was close enough to meeting the requirements outlined by Doenitz.

Hardegen unleashed the first of two torpedoes at the British steamer at 6:49 (EST) on the evening of January 11. The tense submariners waited, breaths drawn, as the torpedo sped toward its target. A malfunction of the torpedo's electric firing mechanism had caused the weapon to be released from its tube three seconds late— would the error doom the attack to failure, wasting one of their precious torpedoes? Ninety-six seconds later their question was answered when the steel fish slammed into the side of the *Cyclops,* just behind the forward funnel. The violent explosion sent the forward stack tumbling into the sea. The frightened passengers and bewildered crew quickly abandoned the steamship for the relative safety of the ship's lifeboats.

Meanwhile, Hardegen was deciding how best to finish off his first victim of the patrol, and what he recorded in his logbook as being the "25th steamer for *U-123.*" But his caution was aroused when he noticed a deck gun on board the *Cyclops.* Disturbed further by the steamer's wireless communication with a destroyer they had encountered several days earlier, Hardegen elected to use another torpedo for the final stroke. At 7:18 P.M. he issued the order to fire the second "eel" out of tube number five. At the instant of impact, the poor steamer's back was broken, sealing her fate. Her bow pointed toward the heavens as she slipped beneath the waves five minutes later. But the *Cyclops* refused to die silently. Hardegen writes vividly in his logbook about how the entire submarine was rocked violently by two "very large detonations" and a "metallic clang," which reverberated throughout his boat. So strong were the explosions that he did not believe they could have been from the ship's boilers. Was the *Cyclops* perhaps carrying munitions?

After watching the *Cyclops* disappear from view, the *U-123* turned eastward, running at high speed toward its assigned patrol area off the New York and New Jersey coastlines. Hardegen was concerned that he had lost too much time in sinking the British steamer and was in danger of missing the opening drumbeat of Operation "Paukenschlag." His worry was for naught, however, for he himself would strike the first blow of the bold operation against the Americans.

First Beat of the Drum: the *Norness*

―――――

It is early on the morning of January 14, 1942, and a dark, overcast night greets the German visitors to the American coast. A heavy sea is running, making things uncomfortable inside the cramped U-boat. At 12:24 A.M. the lookouts sight a light to port. Excitement runs high as the light quickly grows into a sight they have all been waiting for: a large, heavily laden, lone tanker traveling peacefully along, unaware of the dangers about to befall her—a juicy target indeed.

Amazed at the tanker's boldness in displaying her navigation lights, the officers aboard *U-123* are nevertheless thankful; their job will be greatly simplified by the tanker's ignorance. The navigation lights of their prey make her a perfect target, aiding the determination of her course and speed. Lieutenant Hardegen orders his boat forward at 10 knots, running ahead of the tanker for 4000 meters in order to reach a more favorable firing position. Turning back toward his quarry, the lieutenant sits motionless, shielded from view by the dark of night, waiting patiently for his target to come into range.

Damn! The first shot is a miss—there is no telltale explosion following the torpedo run. This is too large a ship to allow to escape. The first "eel" must have been set too deep. But the crew of the tanker remains unalerted—there is still time for a second shot. The U-boat commander orders the next torpedo readjusted to run at a depth of 4 meters before issuing the order to fire again.

"Aiming point, aft of bridge! . . . Fire!"

The torpedo jumps out of its tube and begins speeding toward its target. The seconds seem like hours as the crew of the submarine waits silently, anxiously listening for the expected explosion. Will this shot miss too?

But the torpedo continues its high-speed run, unseen by either the crew of the tanker or the U-boat, its course already determined, its destiny decided. Finally, after 45 seconds the inevitable violent detonation comes. A column of flame 500 feet high erupts into the air, instantly followed by an even higher, black mushroom cloud of smoke and soot. The torpedo's run was precise, its deadly strike breaching the tanker's midship tank at her aftermast, opening it to the sea.

Aboard the surprised tanker, a scene of confusion reigns. The crew on watch are knocked from their feet, while the remainder are rudely awakened from their peaceful slumber as the explosion's concussion throws them harshly from their comfortable bunks to the hard deck. A shower of slippery fuel oil rains down upon the stricken tanker, covering her deck and superstructure in the vicinity of the explosion. Luckily for the ship's crew, however, she has not yet caught fire.

Knowing that his ship is not far from a mine field recently laid down by the United States Army, Captain Harald Hansen is not sure if his vessel has fallen victim to a U-boat's torpedo or has struck a mine. He immediately orders a distress signal sent, realizing that he and his crew will quickly need assistance, regardless of the cause of the explosion.

Over the airwaves flashes the message: "SOS. Have been torpedoed or struck mine, 40 nm west of Nantucket Lightship. *Norness*."

A few minutes later, Captain Hansen's lookouts spot the low silhouette of a German submarine in the gloom near their ship, waiting to complete its deed; this is the result of no mine!

"Abandon ship!" orders Captain Hansen.

The crew of the *Norness* struggles to lower the boats in the dark. The seas are rough, and the boat tackle has been soaked with slippery fuel oil thrown onto the deck by the torpedo's explosion, making the operation both difficult and hazardous. Two Norwegian seamen, Kaare Reinertsen and Egil Bremseth, slip while attempting to lower one of the lifeboats. The boat falls into the dark sea below, carrying the two seamen with it. They are not seen again.

Meanwhile, Captain Hansen and seven of the crew manage to successfully lower the ship's motor launch. Twenty-four other crewmen launch and man another of the ship's lifeboats, while another six cling to a raft they free from the doomed vessel. The motor in the launch will not start; the men desperately paddle the heavy boat away from the tanker, fearing that the U-boat will soon fire again. They watch huddled in silence as the German raider slowly circles their ship.

Back on board *U-123*, the wireless operator has intercepted the *Norness*' distress signal, providing Lieutenant Hardegen with the name of his first victim of Operation "Paukenschlag." Consulting his ship register, he finds she has a tonnage of 9577 British tons—a fine prize indeed! She is not finished yet, however, and another shot will be necessary. Taking careful aim at the ship's bridge, Hardegen sets the torpedo in tube number five to run at a depth of 3 meters. Once again the order to fire is given. After running for 107 seconds, the third torpedo strikes home, directly under the tanker's bridge, causing another violent explosion that results in an incredible pillar of flame reaching high into the night sky. The ship's bridge collapses all at once and falls into the sea.

The crew of the U-boat marvels at the incredible scene of destruction they have created. The tanker still sits on an even keel, burning brightly in the darkness against a black, star-filled sky. Nearby, the crew of the *Norness* watches in dismay as their faithful vessel burns out of control. As the U-boat passes closely nearby, still circling the now-crippled ship, the sailors can hear voices in German coming across the glowing ocean. They huddle low in the boats, fearful that the submarine crew may open fire on them next.

But the Germans are concerned only with the tanker, and ignore her crew in their small, frail boats. The huge ship is still not sinking, and one more shot will be needed to send her to the bottom. Fired from tube number six, another torpedo begins its high-speed run. Seconds turn into minutes, and still there is no explosion. Damn it, another miss! Only 2000 meters from the stationary target, a mistake in calculations seems impossible to the German commander. Perhaps the "eel" ran too deep, passing directly under the tanker's keel.

Frustrated, Lieutenant Hardegen painfully acknowledges that he must sacrifice yet another torpedo to finish off the ship. Once again he takes his targeting sights, setting the fish in tube number two to run shallower. He fires for the fifth time in the attack, and silently prays that this shot will finish her. After only 26 seconds, the final torpedo strikes home directly in the ship's engine room. The deck is blown off as a huge tower of flame erupts from the mortally wounded vessel. She finally begins to sink by the stern, settling until only her bow remains visible, with nearly 100 feet of her forward section protruding vertically from the once again dark sea. Here she remains, her bow stubbornly clinging to the surface. Hardegen is amused at the navigational hazard he has left in the middle of the American shipping lanes, and stops to note it in his war diary before proceeding westward toward Ambrose Channel in search of his next victim.

Left behind, the crew of the *Norness* find themselves in the hands of a heavy winter sea in their small boats, far from the safety of land. During the long winter night, the boats become separated. The seven seamen in the motor launch with Captain Hansen are forced to bail throughout the night just to keep their small boat afloat, fighting to keep the heavy seas out of their craft. Thirteen hours after taking to the lifeboats they are sighted by the fishing trawler *Malvina D.* out of New Bedford, Massachusetts, which picks up the exhausted sailors.

Meanwhile, the other lifeboat and the raft have been sighted by an army patrol plane, along with the tanker's bow, which still protrudes vertically from the sea. A Navy destroyer and a Coast Guard vessel are dispatched to pick up the survivors, who are taken to the Newport Naval Torpedo Station and treated for exposure.

The eastern seaboard is abuzz with news bulletins and wireless traffic. Reports filter in that a tanker has been torpedoed off the coast by a Nazi submarine. Information is scarce; details are sketchy. The naval authorities refuse any comment. Rumors travel up and down the coast at lightening speed. Finally, the authorities confirm the disturbing news: the Panamanian tanker *Norness* has been torpedoed 60 miles southeast of Montauk Point. Thirty-eight survivors of the 40-man crew have been rescued and brought ashore. Wireless messages are sent across the air waves warning all shipping to beware of German submarines.

But the *U-123* is no longer concerned with the *Norness,* for she is searching the American shipping lanes for the rich targets they hold. At 6:15 A.M., the crew sights a pair of masthead lights to starboard. Afraid of being silhouetted against the rising morning sun, Hardegen orders the boat submerged fifteen minutes later. He cautiously closes on the vessel, hidden from view, until he brings the submarine to within 400 meters of her stern. From this close vantage point, he can clearly make out the vessel's name through his periscope: *Isle of Tenerife.* She is Spanish, 5115 British tons—what a shame! Since Spain is neutral in this conflict, he has no choice but to let her proceed unmolested. The Spanish crew will never know of their close brush with danger.

Afraid of being caught on the surface during daylight this close to the American coast, Hardegen decides to spend the rest of the day submerged, setting a pattern to be followed for the remainder of the cruise. The crew monitors the uncoded radio traffic. They chuckle at the warnings issued by the U.S. Navy to all shipping of their presence, and learn that the bow of the *Norness* still protrudes from the sea. They hear of patrol boats and destroyers being dispatched to the scene of the sinking—the Americans are thoughtful enough to warn them of their pursuers! Later they pick up an SOS signal from the steamer *Dayrose,* 600 miles off Cape Race, Nova Scotia. She is undoubtedly the handiwork of one of their fellow U-boats. The operation is going well.

That night, they once again begin their hunt on the surface. Hardegen navigates his *unterseeboot* closer to land, observing the lights of the many small, coastal fishing boats. Daringly, he brings the large submarine so close to shore that he has only 11 meters of water under her keel—not even enough to cover the conning tower if he should need to take her underwater! Realizing the foolishness of this action, he again moves offshore, searching for the east-west shipping traffic he hopes to disrupt.

Second Strike: The *Coimbra*

January 15, 1942, 1:40 A.M. There is a set of steamer lanterns to starboard. Once again, the brightly burning masthead lights aid the German raiders in determining the vessel's course and speed. As they close silently on the bearer of these beacons, they recognize it as another large tanker making its way peaceably eastward at 10 knots. What good fortune!

After an hour of careful maneuvering to position his boat for a good shot, Lieutenant Hardegen unleashes a single torpedo out of tube number one, from a distance of only 800 meters. The calcula-

The Coimbra *was the second tanker sunk off the East Coast during World War II. Her bow stubbornly protruded above the surface for several days before finally accepting her fate and sinking to the bottom. Photo courtesy of The Peabody Museum, Salem, Massachusetts.*

tions are accurate; the deadly steel fish runs straight and true. After 58 seconds it strikes astern of the tanker's bridge with a terrific explosion. A 600-foot-high pillar of flame and smoke springs upward, lighting the entire sky as if it is daylight. The ship takes an immediate list to port. A distress signal quickly bursts over the airways. It is acknowledged by the Cape Race wireless station, but this is of little comfort to the British seamen aboard the doomed tanker *Coimbra*.

Worried that the incredible explosion must have been seen clear to New York City, Hardegen works quickly to prepare a second shot and finish off his latest victim. He has grown wary now that their presence near the coast is known. A second torpedo from tube number five hits the tanker's hull 150 feet forward of her stern after a 45-second run. Following the loud detonation, the familiar pillar of flame erupts from the tanker, spewing flaming oil high into the sky, before it rains down upon the entire ship.

Aboard the tanker, fires burn ferociously at both impact points. The men scramble to the lifeboats, racing to abandon ship before she

The early morning darkness was shattered by the explosion of two torpedoes on January 15, 1942, as the U-123 *mortally wounded the British tanker* Coimbra. *Drawing by author.*

goes down. They manage to get several of the boats and a couple of rafts over the side. One boat capsizes in the cold December sea, and its occupants cling desperately to its upturned hull. Chief Officer W. L. Pinder, having gone forward on the main deck to assess the damage after the first torpedo hit, finds himself trapped between two raging fires after the second explosion. Taking the only avenue of escape open to him, he jumps overboard into the icy sea. Fortunately for Officer Pinder, the Germans pick this very instant to switch on a searchlight, turning it on the burning tanker in order to view their handiwork. This stroke of luck enables Pinder to locate the capsized lifeboat, lying nearby in the dark sea with 11 men already clinging to it. Together they manage to right the boat and scramble in. The continually breaking swells make it impossible for the men to empty the boat of water, however. Shaken and cold, the 12 sailors huddle down into the water that fills the small boat, savoring its relative warmth, which shields them from the below-freezing air temperature. Nearby, only 15 minutes after the second torpedo hit, the men watch as their burning ship sinks by the stern. Mimicking the *Norness* before her, the *Coimbra*'s stern settles to the ocean floor, her bow jutting gruesomely from the sea at a haphazard angle, exposed to her forward mast.

The icy North Atlantic knows no kindness in the depths of winter, and it is not long before the first of the *Coimbra*'s crew succumbs to the numbing cold. A young, 17-year-old wireless operator is the first to die. Others follow at intervals as the life-draining cold extracts its toll from the men. The *Coimbra*'s captain, second and third officers, four sailors, the bo'sun, and the second wireless operator all slip slowly from the ranks of the living. After seven hours in the water-logged boat, only 2 of its original 12 occupants remain alive: Chief Officer Pinder and the senior wireless operator. But both are fading rapidly, finding it difficult to remain awake as they, too, feel death approaching. Finally, at 9:00 A.M. on January 15, a patrol plane sights the boat and radios its position to the destroyer *Rowen*. Yet rescue will not come for another six hours. Perhaps the sight of the plane instilled enough hope in the men to hang on to life for a few more hours. At 3:00 P.M. the men are finally pulled aboard the destroyer. Four other men are picked up from a raft by another American destroyer; three more survivors are rescued by a third vessel and taken to St. John's, Newfoundland.

Of the entire crew of 46 men, including 4 Navy and 2 Army gunners, there are only 9 survivors left to tell of the sinking. The death toll off the American coast is growing rapidly.

The Drum Beats On

Quite pleased with the half-submerged obstacles he had left in the "Yankee" shipping lanes, Lieutenant Hardegen turned his submarine southward and headed toward Cape Hatteras in search of more enemy shipping. He didn't have to travel far before finding another easy victim, which he ran across on January 17. In the early morning twilight he sighted a deeply laden freighter of about 4000 tons, heading northward at 11 knots. Letting loose his last stern torpedo at 6:01 A.M., he scored a direct hit in the freighter's bridge 57 seconds later. A violent explosion followed, and after the smoke and debris had cleared, all that was visible were the ship's masts protruding from the water. The freighter had sunk in only 30 seconds!

Various authors have concluded, for unknown reasons, that this freighter was the American steamship *San Jose*. This is quite impossible, however, as the *San Jose* was sunk in a collision with the steamship *Santa Elisa* at 8:00 P.M. on the same day—14 hours after Hardegen sank his 4000-ton freighter. The course chart of *U-123* shows the vessel it sank square in the middle of grid CA 5756 (the German naval charts used a grid system for recording positions rather than latitude and longitude). This position is some 80 miles south of where the *San Jose* sank. Just what vessel Lieutenant Hardegen did torpedo on the morning of January 17 is a mystery.

Shortly after midnight on January 18, the *U-123* was again on her nighttime prowl when she sighted lights ahead to port. Shortly after, she heard the detonation of two torpedoes. Hardegen quickly realized that he had just been beaten to the punch by his compatriot Richard Zapp in *U-66*, who had just torpedoed the Standard Oil tanker *Allan Jackson*. "Paukenschlag" was proceeding exactly as planned.

Just after 8:00 P.M. that evening, however, a light to starboard led him to his own war prize. Again a deeply laden freighter of about 4000 tons, heading northward at a speed of 9 knots, demanded his attention. Carefully setting up the torpedo shot, he was undoubtedly upset when the torpedo malfunctioned, heading harmlessly off course. But in the darkness the freighter's crew remained unalerted, giving the crew of the German submarine a second chance. Running ahead of the freighter to carefully set up their second attack, Hardegen closed to within 450 meters before letting loose another of his dwindling supply of torpedoes. After a run of 30 seconds, the deadly steel "eel" slammed violently into the side of the helpless steamship, directly under her smokestack. The huge explosion mortally wounded her, and she quickly sank by the stern, with her bow protruding from the calm sea at a steep angle before disappearing from sight.

Once again the identity of Hardegen's kill is a mystery. Several authors have listed the freighter as being the 4497-ton American freighter *Brazos*. But it is known that the *Brazos* was sunk 150 miles southeast of Cape Hatteras in a collision on January 13, and therefore can't possibly be Hardegen's fifth victim.

Four hours later, yet another steamship presented its silhouette to the hungry German commander, just south of Wimble Shoals, North Carolina. The 5269-ton United States cargo-passenger steamer *City of Atlanta* was destined to become Hardegen's sixth kill of his first American patrol. Boldly closing to a range of only 250 meters, he set a single torpedo to run shallow due to the limited water depth. But the torpedo's depth control was apparently set too shallow, and the steel fish leaped out of the water twice during its high-speed run toward its target. Due to the short range, however, the torpedo required only 15 seconds to reach its mark, and the crew of the steamship never had a chance of spotting it. The torpedo struck home in the steamer's engine room, and she immediately took on a severe list to port. While the German U-boat circled the ship, playing a searchlight on her, she rolled over and disappeared beneath the waves. She had taken only ten minutes to sink, and only 3 of her 47-man crew would survive their ordeal in the clutches of the darkened winter sea.

Leaving the scene of his latest sinking, Hardegen soon sighted the lights of no less than five ships traveling in a column. Recognizing the first in line as a tanker, but estimating her size as only 2000 tons, he elected to save his two remaining torpedoes for bigger prey and attack the tanker with shell fire. After scoring at least six hits on the vessel, and observing that she had taken on a slight list to port, the Germans turned to chase the other ships in the column, which had since hurried off into the night. Hardegen was particularly interested in one large freighter that he had estimated at 6000 tons. Giving chase, he soon discovered that his quarry had already run some 15 miles ahead during his gun battle with the tanker. But luck was with the German commander tonight, and shortly there appeared ahead a freighter of an estimated 5000 tons, heading northward. As he set his sights on this new target, the tanker he had just shelled sent out an SOS message over the airwaves, serving to identify his victim as the 8207-ton tanker *Malay*. Surprised at the tanker's large size, he elected to shoot one torpedo at the rapidly approaching freighter, and then return and use his last "eel" to finish off the *Malay*.

Somewhat hampered by broken cooling tubes feeding one of his diesel engines, Hardegen nevertheless unleashed a single torpedo from a range of 450 meters—it struck the freighter *Ciltvaira* directly under her smokestack, breaking the ship in two with a terrific explosion. With her back broken she was doomed, and so the *U-123* came about and made for the crippled tanker, which had just broadcast that she had extinguished her fires and was under way again. Overtaking the limping ship, he shot his final torpedo, managing to hit her directly in the engine room. Believing she was mortally wounded and having used up his supply of torpedoes, the German commander felt it was time to retire from the shoal waters in which he had been operating—the water here would barely cover the submarine's conning tower were he to submerge!

Heading eastward on a course of 90°, toward deeper water, he shortly encountered a large "tanker" which, to his surprise, turned in chase and tried to ram his U-boat! Unable to dive because of the shallow water, he resorted to zigzagging away on the surface, and only his slightly superior speed saved the submarine from its pursuer. Later, the Germans learned that the large "tanker" was the Norwegian whaleship *Kosmos II,* of 16,966 tons. They also picked up a wireless message from the *Malay* crying: "SOS. Sinking rapidly, next ship please hurry, torpedoed, sinking." Leaving the American coast and heading for the open sea, Lieutenant Hardegen noted in his war diary that he had sunk a total of "8 ships, among them 3 tankers with 53,860 British tons." His estimate would prove to be both optimistic and premature, however. His claim assumed that the tanker *Malay* would sink, although in fact, she managed to limp into port under her own power, despite the pounding she had taken from both shell fire and the torpedo hit. Yet his tonnage claim was still not complete. Even without torpedoes, he managed to sink two more vessels in the open Atlantic en route to Germany. On January 25, he shelled and sank the 3044-ton steamship *Culebra,* and on the following day he sent the 9231-ton tanker *Pan Norway* to the bottom, also by artillery fire. This boosted his claimed tonnage to a total of 66,135 tons, comprising ten ships (again, we must subtract the *Malay*, as she did not sink). Still, his actual total of nine ships sunk was a tremendously successful cruise, and he returned home bent on persuading Admiral Doenitz to send every available boat to the American hunting grounds.

After the War

———

The close of the Second World War left the ocean floor off the East Coast of the United States littered with shipwrecks. Broken and twisted hulks lie hidden deep beneath the waves, remnants of the war's closest battleground. Even before the war had ended, the U.S. Hydrographic Office began publishing a set of navigation charts marking the location of all known shipwrecks. The charts listed nearly 200 wrecks along the East Coast from New York to Cape Hatteras by the end of the war, although not all were sunk as a result of the conflict. The government demolished or cleared any that

Ralph Ziobrowski pauses to have his photograph taken next to the one blade of the Coimbra's *propeller which still protrudes from the sandy ocean floor. Photo by author.*

presented a hazard to navigation, and most quickly faded from the public consciousness. Only fishermen cared enough to know their exact whereabouts, for the wrecks quickly became artificial reef sites for a wide variety of marine life, as well as a hazard to commercial trawlers, whose expensive nets became hung up on their battered remains. But for all intents and purposes, their silent slumber remained largely undisturbed.

In 1963, the interest of Dr. Henry Frey, a consultant in physical oceanography, was aroused by reports from local fishermen and sport divers. The fishermen reported that small oil slicks were frequently sighted in the vicinity of the wreck of the British tanker *Coimbra*, some 30 miles south of the Long Island coastline. Dr. Frey's interest quickly grew as he probed further into the situation and discovered that there were more than 100 tankers sunk during the war along the coast from Maine to Texas. His concern stemmed from the pollution threat posed by the sunken vessels, some of which might still contain large quantities of their potentially damaging cargo. Two years after learning of the oil slicks near the *Coimbra*, Frey himself made a bounce dive on the wreck to inspect her condition firsthand. Dr. Frey had begun what would become an uphill and ultimately unsuccessful campaign to thwart the potential ecological threat of the sunken tankers.

Early in 1967 several large oil slicks mysteriously appeared off the East Coast. The two largest appeared off Cape Cod, Massachusetts, and Cape May, New Jersey. At first it was suspected that these were the result of oil tankers cleaning their tanks offshore. This theory was later discounted when an investigation indicated that there had been no tankers in the area at the time. The source of these slicks remained a mystery.

Four years after Frey began his investigation, the government finally took notice. It took the grounding of the American-owned tanker *Torrey Canyon* off southwest England on March 18 and the resulting pollution disaster to make things happen. Only then did the U.S. Congress authorize funds for a study of the sunken tankers. The study was conducted jointly by the Departments of the Interior and Transportation, and the Corps of Army Engineers. Ocean Systems Corporation was contracted to do the diving, and the U.S. Coast Guard provided the transportation and support platform for the operation in the form of the Coast Guard cutter *Sweetgum*.

During the study divers were sent down to examine four different vessels: the tanker *Gulftrade,* sunk by *U-588* on March 10, 1942; the *R. P. Resor,* sunk on February 28, 1942, by *U-578;* the tanker *Varanger,* torpedoed by *U-130* during Operation "Paukenschlag" on January 25, 1942; and, finally, the *Coimbra.* The resulting final report concluded that there was too little oil remaining in the wrecks to pose a significant pollution threat. In fact, of the four wrecks examined, oil was found only in the *Coimbra.* This is certainly not surprising, since both the *Gulftrade* and *Resor* lie in fairly shallow water and are quite broken up. While the *Varanger* lies somewhat deeper, her tanks are, for the most part, torn or corroded open. On the *Coimbra,* however, only four of her tanks were found to be open and accessible to divers—the remainder were closed to the sea and uninspectable. Trace amounts of oil were found in the open portions of the wreck, but the status of the remaining tanks was unclear as efforts to examine them proved unsuccessful. The bow was found to be impenetrable, and an effort to drive a steel tube through the hull plating with a stud gun to sample the tanks' contents failed due to the thickness of the hull plating. Oil was found to be escaping from the sunken vessel "at the rate of about a cupful an hour, but Coast Guard officials said it posed no threat to the Eastern beaches." This was the deepest of the four wrecks examined, and may well be why she is in better condition than the others. If this indeed indicates a trend, there may be even more oil present in deeper wrecks such as the *Norness.*

Dr. Frey disagreed with the report's findings, however, and continued his campaign. He spent much of the early seventies giving lectures on the subject and attempting to secure funding for a study of the potential pollution disaster he felt was waiting just offshore. In 1976, with the assistance of the Coast Guard, he conducted a study of the surface currents in the vicinity of the *Coimbra* to determine the area of impact should significant quantities of oil suddenly be released from the wreck. Dropping waterproof, self-addressed "drifter cards" at the wreck site each month, he plotted their location as they washed ashore, and he conducted a computer simulation of the local ocean currents. The study told Frey the projected impact area. Depending on the prevailing winds, the affected area would be

On the surface over the wreck site, small oil slicks such as these are a common sight and an indication that some oil definitely remains inside the sunken tanker Coimbra. *Photo by author.*

either the southern New England region, including Cape Cod, Martha's Vineyard, and Nantucket, or the southern coast of Long Island, near Jones Beach. Despite more than a decade of public outcry by Dr. Frey, however, nothing was ever done about this threat to our shoreline, other than the brief study conducted in 1967.

Just how much of a threat is posed by these derelict tankers is still questionable. They have now lain on the ocean floor for almost 50 years, with no ill effect on our coast. Yet it is a certainty that oil still remains inside their submerged compartments. As any fisherman or diver who has visited the wreck of the *Coimbra* will tell you, small oil slicks can almost always be found over her grave site. On a calm day, small brown globules of oil can be seen slowly bubbling to the surface from the depths. The globules slowly spread into circular, rainbow-colored "puddles" several feet in diameter, which then join together and form a long, thin slick stretching into the distance with the prevailing current. The *Coimbra* was carrying lubricating oil, and

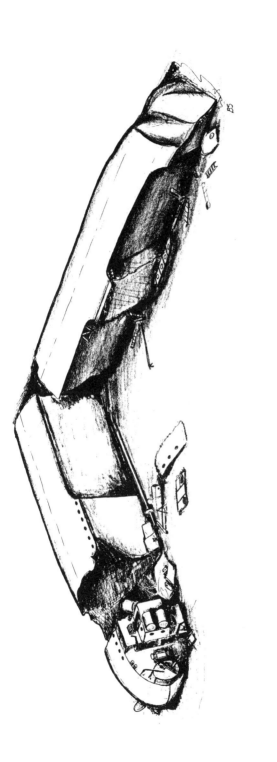

Today the Coimbra lies on her starboard side under 180 feet of water. Her hull is broken at each of the torpedo impact points, which has allowed some of her cargo to escape over the years since her sinking. The unbreached compartments still hold oil, however, which will eventually be released as the ship's hull slowly succumbs to the inevitable corrosive action of the harsh ocean. Drawing by author.

Inside the Coimbra's *galley, an ocean pout inhabits a large stainless steel sink, none the wiser to the violent history behind his comfortable home. Photo by author.*

not the now-familiar "black crude" associated with most modern oil spills. The slicks are a constant reminder of what lies below, and the only real question is just how much oil remains. It now leaks and dissipates slowly, causing no apparent damage to the environment. But should the ship's hull break open suddenly from the effects of

A tank inspection hatch is crushed against the sea floor by the weight of the steel hull above it. How much oil still remains inside the tank compartments of the wreck, and when will it finally escape? Photo by author.

corrosion and winter storms, the oil that remains would be released all at once. It is a race between the escaping oil and the deterioration of the hull, with possibly dire consequences for the environment depending on the winner.

The *Coimbra* lies on her starboard side under 180 feet of water. Her hull is broken at each of the torpedo impact points, forming three, fairly intact sections. The shortest of the three pieces is the extreme stern, whose deck lies heeled over approximately 80° to starboard. Part of the superstructure is still in place, including the stern gun that Lieutenant Hardegen made a note of in his war diary. Just forward of the stern section lies the midship piece of the wreck, intact to a point approximately 40 to 50 feet aft of the center-island bridge. It lies inclined somewhat farther to starboard at an angle of about 100°.

The rim of a porthole is all that remains of the walls in the stern deckhouse, now frequented by hundreds of bergalls and an occasional school of pollock. Photo by author.

Forward of this second break in the hull, the remainder of the ship runs intact all the way to her bow, which is somewhat crumpled and twisted, and heeled over so far that it lies nearly upside down on the sandy bottom.

It is difficult to ascertain the condition of her internal tanks. In the extreme stern, her hull is but an empty shell. All the internal appointments of her crew's quarters have slid to the lower, starboard side of the wreck. Here, amidst a confused pile of rubble, divers found her galley implements, including a few unbroken pieces of china bearing a small, blue flag emblazoned with a single letter "S." This apparently represents the initials of her owners, the Socony-Vacuum Company, Ltd. There were no oil tanks in this part of the ship.

At both of the torpedo impact points, the oil tanks are open to the sea and empty. Between the hull breaks, little can be concluded about

Knowing that two helm wheels had already been recovered from the Coimbra, *diver Phred Cichowski was surprised to find this wooden wheel buried deep in the ship's stern. Photo by author.*

A lonely stairway lies alongside the bow of the sunken tanker Coimbra. *Photo by author.*

the presence or absence of oil inside. The exterior of the hull is in excellent condition, with no apparent breaches. Along the sand, several of her tank inspection hatches can be seen, bent and distorted by the weight of the ship's hull. While open to the sea, the hatches now lie at the bottom of the tank since the ship lies on her starboard side. This effectively blocks this escape route for the lighter-than-water oil.

Some years ago, diver Rick Jaszyn discovered firsthand that the wreck still contained at least some of her once-precious cargo. Searching the wreck for portholes, one of the most sought-after artifacts among wreck divers, he located one still in place on its hinges. Upon opening it, he was treated to a small geyser of brown oil, which engulfed him in its sudden escape. Rick was momentarily blinded by the slippery liquid, but managed to make his way safely back to the surface and the dive boat. There he became the object of humorous but good-natured jokes as he was hosed off before being allowed back on board.

The *Coimbra* has been extensively explored by sport divers over the past decade. Many portholes, which are of highly polished brass and make a rather striking addition to any artifact collection, have been recovered from the wreck. Two telegraphs were wrested from the stern superstructure by divers Keith Wipprecht and John Rangos, and Bill Nagel was lucky enough to find two helms on the wreck, both of which he brought to the surface. Knowing that the *Coimbra* had already yielded two helms, Phred Cichowski was more than a little surprised when he poked his head through a corroded hole in the afterdeck, just below the stern gun platform, and discovered yet another helm! After spending several dives laboriously hacksawing through the wheel's shaft, he too brought up his prize.

Diving the wreck in 1989, I was confused to find the muzzle of the stern deck gun pointing down and aft. My memory seemed to be failing me, for I remembered it pointing forward. Puzzled, I nevertheless corrected my drawing of the wreck and forgot the incident. Later, upon searching through my slide collection, I discovered some photographs I had taken of the gun in 1988; sure enough, the barrel was pointing forward! Somehow, the gun had mysteriously moved over the long winter, and was now pointing toward the ship's stern. Was this the prank of a resident ghost?

For now, the old tanker lies quietly on the ocean bottom, visited frequently by fishermen and occasionally by curious divers. Her location is clearly marked, however, by the thin slick of lubricating oil continuously oozing from her hull. No one knows exactly how much oil remains in her holds, or how long her heavy, steel hull will resist the relentless deterioration of the sea water in which she lies. Tragically, the *Coimbra* may someday make headlines once again.

The "West Wreck"

‗‗‗‗
‗‗‗‗
‗‗‗‗
‗‗‗‗
‗‗‗‗
‗‗‗‗
‗‗‗‗
‗‗‗‗
‗‗‗‗
‗‗‗‗
‗‗‗‗
‗‗‗‗
‗‗‗‗
‗‗‗‗
‗‗‗‗
‗‗‗‗

Dive stories can sometimes be like fish stories, the proverbial one-that-got-away type, that is. Often-told stories by members of "the old gang," those divers who were diving these same wrecks 20 or more years ago when scuba diving was in its infancy, describe picturesque, virgin wreck sites beyond belief. They tell tales of swimming about untouched shipwrecks, being able to pick a porthole stamped with any number they fancied. They tell of mounds of china stretching as far as the eye could see, and of sending up goody-bags filled with these treasures. Such tall tales often extend to secret wreck sites, which were explored by no one but the tale's teller. These ancient shipwrecks lie undisturbed on the bottom, waiting for someone adventurous enough to visit them and discover the secrets they still hold. The yarn that reached us about the "West Wreck" would turn out to be just such a tale.

The "West Wreck" was also called by another name, "The Upside-Down Wreck." She was an obscure wreck; her identity and even her existence was unknown to most. To local fishermen she was merely a snag where an abundance of fish could sometimes be found. But a local contingent of old-time divers told us of a huge, upside-down hull lying on the bottom, far offshore in deep water. Our interest was immediately piqued. Inquiring further, we were even more intrigued after hearing that the wreck was virtually unexplored. The divers who told us of the vessel had dove on her only once, and they had conducted merely a cursory examination of her remains on a short, five-minute "bounce dive," done with the limited air supply available in single tanks. The story they told us, however, commanded our attention instantly with fantastic dreams of glory and adventure. Rumors even surfaced that she was actually a lost aircraft carrier, thus justifying the reportedly huge size of her hull.

Here was a tale of an untouched wreck, intact but upside down on the ocean floor. Every diver dreams of finding and diving such a virgin site. Passed over by generations of previous adventurers, all her prizes would be lying about, waiting to be reclaimed by her first visitors. Urgency becomes the order of the day. No matter that she has lain there for countless decades, we must dive her, and soon! No telling who might be planning a similar adventure while we sit idly dreaming of glory.

Knowing little more than has been related here, we decreed that on our upcoming charter on the *Seeker*, we would attempt to locate and explore the mysterious "West Wreck." Not that this decision was without dissent, however; there are always differing views about what ships we should visit—everyone has their own favorite wreck, ongoing projects, and visions of triumph and conquest. Some believed that this wreck was a shadowy phantom and didn't exist at all. Others felt that their time would be more profitably spent working a known wreck where they were assured of a good dive, if not an artifact to bring home for their efforts. Still others had been involved in more than enough searches for the ever-elusive "virgin wreck," and claimed that they had learned their lesson.

But those of us running the charter insisted, and our destined appointment with this mysterious entity was sealed.

The trip offshore was uneventful, and for once we were blessed with reasonable weather. Upon arriving at the loran coordinates given to us, we anxiously crowded into the *Seeker*'s wheelhouse, eyes glued to the video echo sounder in nervous anticipation of what we would find at this remote spot in the ocean, so far off the New Jersey coastline. Almost immediately we began to pick up wreckage far below—the wreck indeed existed! Soon there appeared larger shadows on the fathometer; not as large as we had anticipated, but plenty big enough to fuel our enthusiasm. She appeared to rise off the bottom a good 25 to 35 feet. This must certainly be a good size ship!

Dropping the dive boat's grapnel, we snagged the wreck on the first try. A query for volunteers to tie in the anchor line received no takers, however. Perhaps the bottom depth of 210 feet, as read on the boat's fathometer, had a part to play in this absence of enthusiasm. No matter, Pete Guglieri and I, having conceived the idea of visiting what we envisioned as a pristine artifact haven would be more than glad to have first pick at the vast selection of goodies lying below. Descending a mere 210 feet to tie the grapnel into an unknown debris field was a side issue; we would beat all the other divers to the wreck and find ourselves on a virtual shopping spree among all the objects of a wreck diver's dream!

Reaching the end of the anchor line after a long descent, we found both our depth gauges and our nitrogen-fogged brains telling us that we were indeed at a depth of 210 feet. Clumsily dragging the heavy grapnel over to a large pile of debris, we (quickly??) tied the line's terminal chain around a huge wooden beam. Surely this foot-square timber would moor the dive boat securely in place.

Having accomplished this task, we were now free to have our pick of all the prime artifacts lying about. But where were they? Around us appeared only heavily overgrown wooden timbers, strewn about in haphazard disarray. Of course! We must have been dropped on the edge of the wreck; the main hull and its artifacts must be lying only a short distance away.

Moving away from the safety of the anchor line, somewhat overcome by nitrogen narcosis (but this is the fun kind of narcosis, I thought!), we swam off in an optimistic search for the main wreckage and the incredible cache of treasures that we knew it held. Around and around we swam. We kicked off a hundred feet or so in this direction; finding nothing, we retraced our steps and headed off toward a new section of wreckage. After finding this trek unproductive, we returned to our starting point and headed off in yet another direction. All we could seem to find were piles of ancient wooden wreckage, indiscernible in form or purpose after many decades of decay, lying deep in the harsh ocean. Our bottom time was rapidly disappearing at this depth, and we suddenly realized that we didn't really know exactly where the anchor line was!

Such dawning realizations at great depths with so little bottom time remaining can always be counted on to induce a rush of adrenaline—just in case you aren't nervous enough just swimming around at 210 feet. No matter that you have come fully prepared with a decompression reel, wound with hundreds of feet of line in anticipation of just this situation. There is always that fearful twinge in the pit of your stomach as you realize you have blown your dive plan and must now ad-lib your critical ascent back to the surface.

As if the nitrogen god was teasing us, we wandered about anxiously for a minute or two before we finally stumbled across the anchor line that we ourselves had tied in only minutes before. We glanced at each other in humorous horror; the huge wooden beam to which we had secured the dive boat was bouncing violently up and down, like some deadly yo-yo. Dodging the dangerously swinging timber, we scooted up the anchor line toward the surface with no regrets—this much-anticipated dive had turned out to be a disaster!

An hour later, with all but two of the divers back on board, individual dive accounts were laughingly exchanged as we found that our experience was not unique. A quick survey of the players in this saga is most revealing:

> Keith Wipprecht: "Regarding the 'West Wreck,' I think that we can leave it for the 'west' of the divers!"
> Steve Gatto: "I think its a set of (loran) numbers which can be forgotten."
> Gene Howley: "The rocks were very, uh, ...uh, ...very interesting rock formations."

After this brutal assessment of our selection of dive sites, all that remained was a vote on where we should go next. A quick poll of those on board found an overwhelming landslide for the *Bidevind*, one of the wrecks closest to our present location.

This decided, one of the boat's crew dressed and descended to free us from what we had concluded must be an old, broken barge. But, alas, we had forgotten two players in this as yet uncompleted drama. Lou Sarlow and his dive buddy had not yet surfaced and, just as we seemed to have written off this exploration as another vain search for that elusive, virgin wreck site, Lou clambered back on board.

Excitedly he told us of finding three portholes at the very end of his dive; but he had run out of time and had to leave them behind. All on board gathered around as he related his story. Exploring the same wreckage as we had, he alone had stumbled across evidence that this might be a *real* ship after all, and that it might hold promise for *real* artifacts. Reluctantly we told him that the anchor already had been freed, and that the boat would shortly be heading to the *Bidevind*.

But for this final twist we could have written off this wreck, chalked it up as one more sunken barge not worth our explorations. Now, however, there will always be a lingering doubt as to her worth as a dive target. Not one of us will be able to safely say that she was fully explored, that she does not warrant another visit. Is it possible that she really is that fabled but elusive wreck, holding treasures beyond description? Only a return visit to thoroughly explore her will answer this question for certain. Such indeed is the allure of wreck diving.

Beyond

Reach?

———

———

———

———

———

———

———

———

———

———

———

———

———

———

———

———

The diving depicted up to this point has been deep, beyond the normal limits recognized by the sportdiving community. The wrecks we have explored lie in depths ranging from 150 to 250 feet, although very few divers have actually visited the extreme depths of this range. Only two of the wrecks, the *Andrea Doria* and the USS *Wilkes-Barre*, lie in waters as deep as 250 feet, and they come to within 170 and 140 feet of the surface, respectively.

But where exactly is the limit? How deep can amateur divers actually go before the hazards become too great, the risks unacceptable? While this largely becomes a matter of individual ability and desire, there are, of course, certain physical limitations. Using only ordinary air, a diver is theoretically limited to a depth of approximately 300 feet. Beyond this, the partial pressure of oxygen in the diver's lungs reaches a level at which it actually becomes toxic. The first signs of oxygen toxicity, or an "O_2 hit" as it is called, involve muscular twitching, nausea, vomiting, dizziness, tunnel vision, hearing difficulty, and even convulsions. Such symptoms underwater would quickly lead to drowning, unless outside help was found. It is rather ironic that oxygen, which is so necessary in the maintenance of human life, can also be the cause of death. This theoretical limit is not some magic threshold that, once crossed, will instantly lead to convulsions and death; it is, rather, a danger zone where the risk of oxygen toxicity is imminent. As with all biological phenomena, individual limits vary from person to person. It is also a time- and pressure-dependent phenomenon, and lung damage can even occur from breathing pure oxygen at sea level for periods in excess of 24 hours.

The other limitation involved with the use of ordinary air at extreme depth is the rapid increase in the effects of nitrogen narcosis, which quickly become unmanageable beyond approximately 200 feet. As explained earlier, nitrogen narcosis becomes more pronounced at greater depths, and at some point reaches a level at which the diver becomes dangerous to himself and anyone with him. This also is largely a matter of individual susceptibility.

Commercial divers have overcome these limitations by altering the composition of their breathing gases, and they quite routinely dive to 800 feet or more. By reducing the amount of oxygen in the breathing mixture, the depth that can be reached before approaching the limits of oxygen toxicity can be extended. At the same time, helium is substituted for some or all of the nitrogen present in the mix. An inert gas, helium lacks the narcotic effects of nitrogen at high pressure. But even helium begins to have strange effects on the body at extreme depths. Beyond approximately 450 feet, helium begins to precipitate what is known as High Pressure Neurological Syndrome (HPNS). It begins with tremors and progresses to lapses in consciousness at depths in excess of 900 feet. In animal experiments at even deeper depths, it has led to convulsions and even death. This syndrome is not well understood and is currently the limiting factor in extremely deep diving. Still, research continues, and recent advances have placed man even deeper in the ocean by utilizing hydrogen mixes as a breathing medium, although this is still highly experimental.

Another added complication is that the departure from using air as a breathing mixture invalidates the use of the U.S. Navy Standard Air Decompression Tables. The substitute gases used in the breathing mixture have a different density and, therefore, diffuse at different rates into and out of body tissues. The result is that different decompression tables must be used. A further complication results from the fact that helium transfers heat approximately six times faster than air. Thus, a diver is rapidly chilled by the heat lost through his lungs into the helium mixture he is breathing. This is usually overcome by the use of heated suits, supplied with hot water through an umbilical to the surface.

With advances in technology and further understanding of human physiology, diving depths have been greatly extended beyond the limits of air diving, but only at the cost of greater complexity and expense. Helium is expensive, as is the equipment needed to mix it and other gases in the exact proportions required to achieve a proper breathing mixture. While the technology and methods are available to those interested, the financial expenditure and operational complexity involved generally precludes the use of these methods by amateur divers.

Of what use would such technology be to us as divers if its use were, in fact, practical? What reason would we have for venturing to such great depths? The answer is the same as the response to more elementary questions, such as why we dive to depths in excess of the sportdiving limits, or why we dive at all. Why did man first venture into the depths of the sea? There is an inexplicable force within all of us that draws us to the unknown, a force that drives us to venture forth and explore what is unseen and unfamiliar. That same force compels us to send planetary probes to the far reaches of the solar system, or to send a bathyscaphe seven miles down into the deepest known ocean trench. In all of us there is a part that is, as described by Captain Jacques Yves Cousteau, "the expression of a civilization in which man requires much more than just his daily bread."[1]

Such longings within me form the impetus for the final chapter of this book. The speculation of using advanced diving techniques to seek out and explore a multitude of shipwrecks that have, without doubt, lain unseen by human eyes since the day they bade goodbye to the surface world stimulates that deep hunger for adventure and knowledge that is within all of us. The shipwrecks whose stories follow are deep, yet not so deep that they are easily dismissed as being impossible to dive upon. The technology exists to explore them; indeed, some are even reachable at the extreme limits of air scuba diving, although it would certainly be a hazardous undertaking. They are there, and they beckon to us to be explored; but they lie at the very limit of the envelope. Are they "Beyond Reach?"

[1] Jack McKenney, *Dive to Adventure* (Vancouver, Canada: Panorama Publications Ltd., 1983), 6.

The SS *Texel* and SS *Carolina*

──────

The *U-117*, which sank the steamship *Sommerstad* during World War I, was not the first German submarine to bring the war to the United States coast. Its voyage to the eastern seaboard was in the wake of the highly successful war cruise of one of her sister submarines, the *U-151*. The *U-151*, under the command of Kapitan von Nostitz und Janckendorff, left Kiel, Germany, on April 14, 1918, bound for the coastal waters of the United States. The German commander was intent upon disrupting U.S. coastal shipping, which, until now, had operated in relative freedom despite the European war. She was

A self portrait by the crew of the German submarine U-151 *on their first visit to the U.S. East Coast during World War I. Photo courtesy of National Archives.*

quite successful in this task, returning home only after she had sunk a total of 22 vessels with a combined tonnage of 52,000 gross tons.

More than one-quarter of her victims on this eventful cruise were sunk in a single day, a tragic testimony of the immaturity of the American coastal defenses. On Sunday, June 2, the large U-cruiser sank a total of six vessels some 60 miles off the New Jersey coastline—easily the most productive day of her entire voyage.

By 4:21 P.M. the German commander and his crew had already sunk the small American steamship *Winneconne*, as well as the three coastal coal schooners, *Isabel B. Wiley*, *Jacob M. Haskell*, and *Edward H. Cole*. About an hour after the *Edward H. Cole* was sent to the bottom, and still within sight of her crew in their lifeboat, another steamship sailed into the clutches of the Germans.

The American steamship *Texel*, under the command of Captain K. B. Lowry, was traveling northward from Ponce, Puerto Rico, with a

On June 2, 1918, the U-151 *approaches the three-masted schooner* Isabel B. Wiley, *the first of six ships sunk by the U-boat that day. Photo courtesy of National Archives.*

cargo of sugar destined for New York. Her peaceful voyage was suddenly interrupted, however, when a shell from the German submarine passed over the forward half of the vessel, ricocheting off the water about 200 yards to port. Captain Lowry immediately turned stern to the submarine to present the smallest target to his pursuers, and ordered full speed ahead in an attempt to escape. A second shrapnel shell exploded to the starboard side of the steamship. All this excitement must have gotten the best of poor Captain Lowry, for at this point he claimed a second submarine surfaced ahead of his vessel, blocking his escape route and forcing him to stop his ship. Subsequent study both during and after the war has proved beyond doubt that there was only one German submarine operating off the U.S. coast at this time. The second submarine can be attributed only to the captain's imagination.

After the *Texel* was stopped, two more shells were fired by the U-boat, the first hitting the working boat on the starboard side of the bridge and the second just missing the bridge, flying about 10 feet overhead before striking the water about 100 yards forward of the vessel. After circling the steamship twice, the U-boat came alongside and an officer and three seamen boarded her. The German officer made his way up to the bridge, where he shook Captain Lowry's hand and apologized for having to sink his ship. Such gentlemanly conduct was actually quite common among U-boat commanders at this time. Meanwhile, the other Germans got to work setting bombs on board to sink the American ship. The last of the boats left the *Texel* at 5:10 P.M. Eight minutes later, the bombs planted on board began to explode, and the freighter sank to the bottom in only three minutes. The entire crew of 36 seamen survived their ordeal, reaching Atlantic City, New Jersey, the following day after rowing their small boats all night.

Although the *U-151* had now sunk five ships since dawn, she was not yet done. Forty minutes after the steamship *Texel* had been sent to the bottom, the New York and Puerto Rican liner SS *Carolina* was unlucky enough to steam across the path of *U-151*. The steamship was nearing the completion of her voyage from San Juan to New York with 218 passengers on board, as well as 117 crew and a cargo of sugar. At 5:55 P.M., the *Carolina*'s wireless operator had picked up a message reporting the earlier sinking of the *Isabel B. Wiley,* giving the position of the attack as only 13 miles from their present location. Captain Barber quickly extinguished all lights on his vessel and altered course to due west, ordering his engineer to apply all speed possible. But immediately after altering course, the Captain of the *Carolina* spotted the big U-cruiser off his starboard quarter, about two miles away. A few minutes later, the Germans opened fire on what would soon become their sixth victim of the day. Their first shot fell about 100 yards astern, while the second shell landed about a half-ship's length ahead of the steamer; the third shot fell even closer still. At this point, the Captain decided it best to stop his ship because of the large number of passengers on board. Bringing his vessel to a halt, he hoisted the American ensign along with the signal flags

The American steamship Winneconne *was the second victim of the day for the crew of the* U-151. *She was sunk with bombs planted on board after her crew was first forced to abandon ship. Photo courtesy of National Archives.*

indicating "I am all stopped." As Captain Barber halted his ship, he rescinded his previous order to send an SOS, fearing that the U-boat might resume the shelling if the message was intercepted. His decision was shortly reinforced when his wireless operator informed him that he had received a low power message from the submarine warning, "If you don't use wireless, I won't shoot."

As the submarine approached the *Carolina*, the Captain could see that the German commander was flying the signal "A.B.," indicating that they should abandon ship as quickly as possible. Resistance was useless, and Captain Barber ordered all hands to the boats. In the long-standing tradition of the sea, women and children were put in the lifeboats first, followed by the male passengers and finally the crew. Captain Barber properly left his ship only after ensuring that all hands were off the vessel and the secret and confidential papers on board were destroyed. Leaving the ship's side in the chief officer's boat at about 6:30, he was ordered by the submarine's commander to

The passenger liner Carolina *would certainly make an intriguing dive, but she lies deep and her exact location is as yet unknown. Photo courtesy of Steamship Historical Society, University of Baltimore Library.*

take his boats and head for shore. About 45 minutes passed before the U-boat took further action when she fired three shells into the abandoned vessel. The submarine then slowly circled the sinking liner. The *Carolina* remained on an even keel for about 20 minutes before listing over to port and slowly disappearing from sight. She apparently took about 40 minutes to sink, and the Germans seemed in no rush to send their last victim of the day to the bottom. Perhaps they wanted to enjoy the sight of their final prey's dying gasps for as long as possible, a kind of celebration of the day's success.

About 11 A.M. the following day, the survivors sighted a schooner to the north and sent one of the boats to intercept her. The schooner turned out to be the *Eva B. Douglas*, and the captain of that vessel took all the survivors on board. But all who left the *Carolina* did not survive. During the rough seas encountered during the previous night, one of the lifeboats had capsized with the loss of eight passengers and five crew members. These were the first deaths attributable to U-boats off the American coast.

Both the *Texel* and the *Carolina* lie in deep water off the New Jersey coast. Although their exact location is not known, there are at least four unidentified "fishing snags" in the general vicinity of their sinkings. Is it possible that one of these snags is the remains of the *Texel* or *Carolina*? Both wrecks would make fascinating dives, and you can be sure that no one has ever been there before.

According to the last reported position of the *Texel*, she appears to lie in approximately 260 feet of water, some 60 miles southeast of Atlantic City, New Jersey. She would be an interesting dive because she is a good example of an early steamship. Her condition is unknown, but according to the statement of her captain, part of her superstructure was blown away by the third shell. The captain also stated that she sank three minutes after the bombs placed by the German sailors exploded; she must have been severely damaged by the explosions for her to sink so rapidly.

Lying only six nautical miles away from the *Texel*, according to her final reported position, the liner *Carolina* is also deep, sitting on the ocean floor beneath 250 feet of water. Being a passenger liner, her grave site must abound with prize artifacts, and the first to reach her will, of course, have their pick of what is there. She was also sunk by shellfire, but because she took a full 40 minutes to founder, it is quite possible that her hull is in excellent condition. If so, she will be an even greater challenge: penetrating a sunken ship at this depth would be an extremely hazardous undertaking. It is, of course, possible that her sunken hulk was depth-charged during the Second World War as a suspected submarine, as so often happened to old wrecks after the invention of sonar. If this is the case, she may be little more than another pile of rubble littering the ocean bottom.

Interestingly, the description of the *Carolina*'s sinking given by William Clark in his excellent book *When the U-Boats Came to America* differs significantly from the version cited previously by Captain Barber ("Barbour," according to Clark). In Clark's account, the liner began to settle by the bow after about 20 minutes and then turned over onto her *starboard* side. She then proceeded to sink by the head until she assumed a vertical position, with about 100 feet of the vessel's stern protruding perpendicularly from the surface of the sea.

She hung suspended like this for approximately ten minutes before slowly disappearing from sight. This version of the story also has the U-boat firing a total of six shells into the liner to sink her.

Still further complexity is added to the story by Kapitan von Nostitz und Janckendorff's logbook. By his own account of the action, we find out that the German captain had first tried to torpedo the *Carolina* after the passengers had abandoned the ship. The torpedo went awry, however, zigzagging off into the sea, astray of its intended target. Only after this misfire did the *U-151* proceed to sink the ship by shellfire. The U-boat commander records the use of eight shells in the effort, although it is not clear if this included the three used initially in stopping the vessel.

The *Norness*

_____

The story of the sinking of the Panamanian tanker *Norness*, along with the other exploits of Lieutenant Hardegen and the *U-123*, has been told fully in an earlier chapter. The *Norness* might well be considered as a larger and deeper cousin of the *Coimbra*, Hardegen's second kill of his American cruise.

Sunk 60 miles southeast of Montauk Point, the *Norness* lies deep, hidden 270 feet beneath the cold Atlantic swell. Being so much like the *Coimbra*, both in construction and method of destruction, one can't help but conclude that the *Norness'* hull might be in much the

The sinking of the 9,577 ton tanker Norness *marked the opening blow of Operation "Paukenschlag" and the coming of the German U-boats to the American coast during World War II. Photo courtesy of The Mariners' Museum, Newport News, Virginia.*

same condition as her shallower relative. It took several torpedoes to destroy each of the tankers, and they both lay only partially submerged with their bows awash and protruding from the ocean for some time before finally disappearing. The *Norness,* however, was a much larger ship with half again the gross tonnage of the *Coimbra,* although she was only 70 feet longer. One might reasonably guess that she lies largely intact on her side as does the *Coimbra,* in which case her 65-foot beam could conceivably bring her upper side to within 210 to 220 feet of the surface (allowing for some settling of her hull into the ocean bottom) and, therefore, within striking distance of divers using scuba equipment. The bottom itself, however, consists largely of greenish mud according to the information charted by NOAA (chart no. 12300), and visibility may be very limited near the bottom. Loran numbers reportedly exist for her exact location, and she would be an easy target to find because of her large size. The trip offshore to the area of her remains is a long one, however, and the dive itself unquestionably would be hazardous. But she holds an important distinction in the annals of history: the first ship torpedoed off the United States coast during World War II, signaling the beginning of Operation "Paukenschlag" and the coming of the Nazi U-boat menace to America.

The "Gulhune"

———

This is not a ship's real name, but rather another fanciful designation by an unknown boat captain. In fact, almost nothing is known about this wreck. It has never been dove on, and is just a set of loran numbers lying deep in the very heart of the "mudhole" off the New Jersey coast. Captain George Hoffman has told us of it many times, claiming that the chart recorder tells him that it is a big wreck, coming fairly high off the bottom. Fortunately (or unfortunately), he will seldom entertain the thought of taking us there since, as he puts it, "That's crazy deep!!" She lies in approximately 230 feet of water according to the NOAA charts, and although this is shallower than the other wrecks in this chapter, her depth is not the only hindrance to diving her, for she is located in the eternal night world of the treacherous mudhole. Perhaps she will never be explored, but I know that there are a few, including Captain Hoffman, who would love to know just what lies beneath the set of loran numbers listed under the name "Gulhune."

The *Pan Pennsylvania* and the *U-550*

Early on the morning of April 16, 1944, yet another tanker was at the receiving end of a German torpedo off the American East Coast. *U-550*, under the command of Kapitanleutnant Klaus Hanert, claimed its first and last victim of her short participation in the "Battle of the Atlantic."

The crew of the 11,017-ton American tanker *Pan Pennsylvania* was forced to abandon ship shortly after being hit by the U-boat's single torpedo. Before being able to finish off his first prize of the war, however, Kapitanleutnant Hanert was forced to deal with more

The American tanker Pan Pennsylvania *was the first and only victim of the ill-fated* U-550. *Photo courtesy of The Mariners' Museum, Newport News, Virginia.*

pressing problems. Arriving quickly on the scene of the action, the three destroyer escorts *Gandy, Peterson,* and *Joyce* picked up approximately 60 survivors from the slowly sinking tanker. Just as the last survivors were pulled from the water by the *Peterson,* the *Joyce* reported a sound contact. Quickly closing in for the kill, the destroyer escort dropped a pattern of depth charges. Minutes later, the damaged German submarine shot to the surface. The *Gandy* immediately opened fire on the U-boat, which quickly returned the shellfire in a last desperate attempt to defend herself. Two minutes later, the *Gandy* closed in and rammed the German attacker, damaging herself in the process. Shortly thereafter the *Peterson* opened fire, then closed and fired two shallow-set depth charges from close range. Hopelessly outmatched, Hanert surrendered and began abandoning his boat only nine minutes after the first depth charges were dropped. The *Joyce* picked up 13 survivors of the *U-550,* including Kapitanleutnant Hanert and two officers, before the submarine disappeared beneath the sea 20 minutes later.

During the heat of the action with the submarine, the *Pan Pennsylvania* was set on fire by shells from the destroyer escorts. The

Approximately two hours after the Pan Pennsylvania *was hit by a single torpedo, the* U-550 *was forced to the surface by a depth charge attack mounted by the U.S. Navy destroyer escort* Joyce. *Photo courtesy of Henry Keatts*

tanker was sinking slowly by the stern and burning fiercely. Early on the morning of April 17, she reportedly turned over and was drifting northwest with approximately 100 feet of her bow still showing above the surface; she was still burning. Later that afternoon, the USS *Sagamore* requested permission to sink the burning hulk using gunfire. The request was granted, but after firing 88 rounds of 3-inch shells, 90 rounds of 40mm, 100 rounds of 8mm, and 4 depth charges, she reported that the tanker was still awash and burning, drifting at about one knot. Finally, early on the morning of April 18, a full 48 hours after being torpedoed, the battered tanker was reported sunk, with only burning oil visible on the ocean surface above her. She had drifted nearly 20 nautical miles before finally coming to rest on the ocean floor.

*As the submarine wallowed helplessly on the surface, her crew came out
of the conning tower fighting. Photo courtesy of Henry Keatts.*

*Their fight on the surface was both short-lived and futile. Quickly
realizing their inevitable fate, the crew of the U-550 abandoned ship.
Note that the* Pan Pennsylvania *can be seen burning in the back-
ground. Photo courtesy of Henry Keatts.*

The last had not been heard of the *U-550,* however. On May 5, a Coastal Picket Patrol Boat recovered a body identified only as "Hube" by the markings on his clothing and wearing a German life jacket, in location 39° 51' N, 71° 58' W, approximately 100 miles west of the sunken U-boat. An autopsy revealed that he had died only five days prior to being picked up. The next day, the same Picket Boat found a German escape lung in position 39° 55' N, 71° 44' W. On May 11, another Picket Boat found the body of a second German sailor afloat in a rubber raft in position 40° 12' N, 71° 45' W. He was wearing both a life jacket and a submarine escape lung, and was identified as Wilhelm Flade by markings found on his clothing. It was estimated that the young man was only 17 years old. On May 16, a third body was found in location 40° 28' N, 71° 00' W, also clad in a German uniform, but with no identification. It was determined that he had been in the water for more than 18 days. Although unconfirmed, the evidence would seem to indicate that several crewmen from the *U-550* escaped the wreck *after* she had sunk by using their escape lungs, and perhaps survived for several days afloat in the open ocean.

By its charted position, the wreck of the tanker *Pan Pennsylvania* lies in approximately 220 feet of water, quite reachable using ordinary scuba gear. Her battered and burned remains have not, to date, attracted enough interest to warrant a visit, however. Perhaps this is due to her location far from shore and only 13 nautical miles southeast of the wreck of the *Andrea Doria.* Divers making the long trek offshore have difficulty finding interest in yet another battered tanker when the elegant Italian liner, which met its fate 11 years after the end of the Second World War, is so close by.

Nearby, however, is an untouched prize for U-boat fanatics in the wreck of the short-lived *U-550.* She lies in deep water, however, and a visit to her remains at a depth of 310 feet would require advanced diving techniques. Perhaps someday a future generation of divers will brave the treacherous depths to explore this time capsule from an era when travel on the high seas was far from safe.

Bibliography

Books

Bockstoce, John R. *Whales, Ice, & Men: The History of Whaling in the Western Arctic.* Seattle and London: University of Washington Press, 1986.

Clark, William Bell. *When the U-Boats Came to America.* Boston: Little, Brown and Company, 1929.

deCamp, Michael A. *Wreck Diving.* Los Angeles: Petersen Publishing Co., 1973.

Finckenor, George A. *Whales and Whaling, Port of Sag Harbor, New York.* Sag Harbor, New York: William Ewers-Printers, 1975.

Greenhill, Basil. *The Life and Death of the Merchant Sailing Ship.* National Maritime Musuem, The Ship, vol. 7. London: Her Majesty's Stationery Office, 1980.

Hegarty, Reginald B. *Returns of Whaling Vessels Sailing from American Ports, 1876–1928.* New Bedford, Massachusetts: The Old Dartmouth Historical Society and Whaling Museum, 1959.

Hocking, Charles. *Dictionary of Disasters at Sea During the Age of Steam, 1864–1962.* Lloyd's Register of Shipping, 1969.

Hoffer, William. *Saved! The Story of the* Andrea Doria—*the Greatest Sea Rescue in History.* New York: Summit Books, 1979.

Hoyt, Edwin P. *U-Boats Offshore.* New York: Playboy Paperbacks, 1978.

Keatts, Henry. *Field Reference to Sunken U-Boats.* New York: American Merchant Marine Museum Press, 1987.

McKenney, Jack. *Dive to Adventure.* Vancouver, Canada: Panorama Publications Ltd., 1983.

Mooney, James L., ed. *Dictionary of American Naval Fighting Ships.* Washington, D.C.: Naval Historical Center, 1981.

Moscow, Alvin. *Collision Course.* New York: Grosset & Dunlap, 1959.

National Oceanic and Atmospheric Administration. *Automated Wreck and Obstruction Information System (AWOIS)*, 1986.

Rattray, Jeannette Edwards. *The Perils of the Port of New York*. New York: Dodd, Mead & Company, 1973.

Robotti, Frances Diane. *Whaling and Old Salem*. New York: Fountainhead Publishers, 1962.

Rohwer, Jurgen. *Axis Submarine Successes, 1939–1945*. Annapolis, Maryland: Naval Institute Press, 1968.

Sleight, Harry D. *The Whale Fishery on Long Island*. Bridgehampton, New York: The Hampton Press, 1931.

Stackpole, Edouard A. *The Sea Hunters*. New York: J. B. Lippincott Company, 1953.

Starbuck, Alexander. *History of the American Whale Fishery*. New York: Argosy-Antiquarian Ltd., 1964.

U.S. Department of the Navy, Office of Naval Records and Library, Historical Section. *Publication Number 1: German Submarine Activities on the Atlantic Coast of the United States and Canada*. Washington, D.C.: Government Printing Office, 1920.

Periodicals

Lloyd's Register of Shipping. Various dates.
Merchant Vessels of the United States. Various dates.
The New York Maritime Register. Various dates.
The New York Times. Various dates.

Articles

Centa, Elinor T. "The *Doria* Entertains a Lady." *Skin Diver Magazine*, April 1973, 42–43.

Dickenson, Fred. "The Tantalizing Treasure of the *Andrea Doria*." *Reader's Digest*, November 1967, 151–153.

Dugan, James. "*Andrea Doria*." *Skin Diver Magazine*, August 1974.

Fales, Daniel C. "Sunken Time Bombs Full of Oil." *Popular Mechanics,* November 1967, 97–101, 222.

Giddings, Al. "The *Andrea Doria,* Everest of the Sea." *Skin Diver Magazine,* January 1969, 12–19.

Gimbel, Peter. "Down to *Doria* Again." *Life,* October 28, 1957.

Lord, Walter. "Rescue at Sea." *Life,* August 6, 1956, 18–32.

MacLeish, Kenneth. "Divers Explore the Sunken *Doria.*" *Life,* September 17, 1956, 46–51.

McKenney, Jack. "The Great Underwater Wreck Robbery, An Attempt at Salvaging the *Andrea Doria,*" *Skin Diver Magazine,* January 1970, 12–17, 20, 22.

———. "*Andrea Doria* Caper, Treasure Vault Finally Opened." *Skin Diver Magazine,* January 1974, 44-51.

———. "*Andrea Doria* Caper, Treasure Vault Finally Opened." *Skin Diver Magazine,* February 1974, 56-61.

———. "The Mystery of the *Andrea Doria.*" *Skin Diver Magazine,* March 1976, 48–51, 59.

Parks, Ramsey. "Exploration of the Sunken Liner *Andrea Doria.*" *Skin Diver Magazine,* June 1957.

Roach, Thomas. "Mystery Wreck at Thirty-Three Fathoms." *Skin Diver Magazine,* October 1975.

———. "The Secret of the USS *Bass.*" *Skin Diver Magazine,* October 1977.

Speaking of Pictures, "Camera in a Sea Tomb." *Life,* August 13, 1956, 12-13.

Sup, Stuart Allen. "Forty Fathoms and Oil." *Skin Diver Magazine,* December 1970, 56–58.

Tzimoulis, Paul J. "The Return of *Andrea Doria.*" *Skin Diver Magazine,* December 1964.

Weissmann, Richard. "Wreck of the *Andrea Doria.*" *Oceans,* November 1983, 42–47.

Index
